JAVIER

Welcome To
The Revolution !

Legal Disclaimers

reader's sole responsibility to seek professional advice before taking any action on their part.

Readers results will vary based on their skill level and individual perception of the contents herein, and thus no guarantees, monetarily or otherwise, can be made accurately. Therefore, no guarantees are made.

Forward By Ross Lightle

My introduction to John McCabe was when John, a true believer that investing in yourself is a lifelong process, enrolled in a Lease Option (Rent to Own) class that I was teaching. I have been investing and teaching the Rent to Own strategy for many years to thousands of people. From the very first time I met John I could tell that John was a "systems" guy. John would ask questions during the class that most people would never ask. I could tell that he was trying to see if there was a better way to build the "Rent to Own mousetrap". It takes someone like John to use his unique imagination and skill set to systemize a program and make it "user friendly". With this book, Rent to Own Revolution, John has done exactly that.

John has spent years working in the real estate business. He has seen what works, what doesn't work, what needs to be tweaked and what needs to be cannibalized. He has seen how many investors use the Rent to Own strategy in unethical ways for personal gain. It is refreshing to see a book that addresses this upfront. John wants to bring legitimacy back to the Rent to Own strategy. At its core, the Rent to Own strategy is vendor financing at its very Win-Win-Win best. It protects and benefits all the parties involved when it is structured correctly. Within the pages of this book John has developed a system that takes years of best practices and experiences and assembles them into a step by step process and system that anyone can clearly understand, follow and use.

John understands the frustrations that investors and homeowners face. Whether you are a seasoned veteran or a brand new investor we all face frustrations. Whether it is the frustration of finding the financing to complete the deal or the right tenant once we have the deal. Or maybe it is the frustration and emotional turmoil of a homeowner who is forced to deal with vacancies, late rental payments, evictions and trashed properties. Once we have secured the deal and placed the right tenant, we have the frustration and inconvenience of managing the property. John has dealt with these frustrations personally and lays out a unique and fresh system that makes investing in real estate as painless and stress free as possible. John gives many real life examples throughout the book that are easy to follow. He points out the mistakes he made along the way and provides you with the system so you don't have to make the same mistakes he has made. As Booker T. Washington said; "Success is not to be measured by the position someone has reached in life, but the obstacles he has overcome while trying to succeed." John has overcome many obstacles and is blazing a new path in the Rent to Own business.

Whether you are an owner that wants to increase your cash flow and reduce your risk, an investor that wants a safe, secure investment with great returns, or simply a perspective home buyer that does not currently qualify for traditional financing, then this book and John's system is for you. Then again, you may not be any of the people above but you know someone who is – please pass this valuable information along.

There is no doubt that for John, writing Rent to Own Revolution was a labor of love to help serve as many people as possible who pursue the Rent to Own strategy. I encourage you to join the Rent to Own Revolution!

For you the reader it will be an investment of your time that will be returned over and over!

In respect

Ross Lightle

"Be the Servant You Were Born to Be"

About The Author

Rent To Own Trusted Authority, John A. McCabe, has been a business consultant and real estate investor since 2004 and has leveraged his education and experience into that of Author, Coach, Mentor, Speaker and Systems and Marketing Expert. He is the author of Rent to Own Revolution and the founder of ioffersolutions Real Estate Services Inc. and Rent To Own Revolution Inc.

John has had an impressive career as both a business consultant and real estate investor. Through his implementation of process, procedures, systems and personnel he helped grow a company from $1.5 million to $7 million in just 4 years while dramatically increasing its profit margin. John then started ioffersolutions Real Estate Services and within 4 years had been involved in controlling close to $10 million worth of real estate without ever using his own money or credit.

His unique investment model using Rent To Own provided his investors and homeowners above average returns, all the benefits of investing in real estate with little to no risks to them.

Originally from Windsor, Nova Scotia he studied Business at Acadia University then moved to Edmonton, Alberta where he currently lives and works. John gives credit to his parents, Gary and Shirley McCabe, for his desire to help and serve others, enjoys Fastpitch Softball, Golf and Travelling the World.

Follow The Author

You can follow John A. McCabe through his Social Media accounts.

Facebook.com/JohnAnthonyMcCabe

Facebook.com/ioffersolutions

Facebook.com/RentToOwnRevolution

Twitter.com/JohnAMcCabe

Youtube.com/user/JohnAnthonyMcCabe

Linkedin.com/in/JohnAnthonyMcCabe

Google.com/+JohnMcCabe

FREE Member's Area

To Join the Rent To Own Revolution Member's Area FREE and get accesses to all the latest updates and resources.

Text your name and email to 780-800-7464

OR Visit http://0s4.com/r/RTOMA

OR Scan the QR code

Acknowledgement

The Rent To Own Revolution book, program and services would not have been made possible if it weren't for several people who have influenced me along the way.

First, my parents, Gary and Shirley McCabe. Had it not been for their love and support in whatever I set my mind to, along with raising me to have strong morals, ethics and desire to help and serve others, this book and accompanying services would not be available.

Ross Lightle, my mentor, taught me Real Estate Investing strategies and to operate my business in a very ethical manner. Ross has taught thousands of students over the past 30 years and has been a mentor to almost 800 Real Estate Investors. I owe much of the Rent To Own Revolution to what I learned from Ross.

Heather, my best friend, has provided me with so much over the past 8 years I don't know where to start. Heather is not only my best friend but also an amazing resource for ioffersolutions Real Estate Services Inc. and Rent To Own Revolution Inc. With her 18 years legal experience and several years of property management experience I consider her to be one of my Trusted Advisors in this business. Heather and her Daughter Hannah keep me grounded on a daily basis.

Contents

Section 1: The Revolution   **Page**

Chapter 1 Introduction to the Revolution   14

Chapter 2 Riding the Training Wave   34

Chapter 3 What Options do Home Owners Have?   64

Section 2: 5 Reasons to Rent to Own

Chapter 4 Access to Equity   91

Chapter 5 Sell Your Home for Top Dollar   120

Chapter 6 Someone Else Pays Mortgage   144

Chapter 7 Someone Else Pays Repairs   160

Chapter 8 Cash Flow is King   177

Section 3: How to Rent to Own a Home

Chapter 9 Rent to Own Steps Part One   193

Chapter 10 Rent to Own Steps Part Two   213

Chapter 11 Additional Rent to Own Services   239

Appendix

i Frequently Asked Questions   259

ii Questions You Should Ask   268

References   280

Section 1: The Revolution

CHAPTER 1

THE REVOLUTION

"One of the great liabilities of history is that all too many people fail to remain awake through great periods of change. Every society has its protectors of status quo and its fraternities of the indifferent who are notorious for sleeping through revolutions. Today, our very survival depends on our ability to stay awake, to adjust to new ideas, to remain vigilant and to face the challenge of change."— Martin Luther King Jr.

There is a revolution about to take place that many people don't know about. As a result of the banking industry getting tighter on qualifying, many people are seeking help getting into home ownership. This dramatic rise, along with every successful and somewhat successful investor creating an education program trying to educate investors on making money in real estate investing and doing no money down strategies, has over populated the market with newbies and shady investors who only care about the money and not about making a difference. In today's environment of full disclosure, honesty, integrity, and being authentic, tenant buyers are demanding more and a revolution is about to start.

This book is about my four year journey in the rent to own business building a system, processes, and procedures that are designed to truly set the tenant buyer up for success while at the same time helping the homeowner maximize the money they make on their home. This was always my intention done with the highest of integrity, full disclosure, and honesty. Many times, they have cost me deals or opportunities but I always felt good and right about what I did. For those who know me, it has always been my nature to help others.

If you are looking to sell your home but don't want to deal with a Realtor, you are not alone. Many people are trying to go it alone when looking to sell their house. So many people are frustrated with Realtors that for sale by owner companies have grown dramatically. These companies offer you services without Realtor commissions. Another form of business that has appeared recently because people are fed up with real estate agents is the discount brokerage. These brokerage firms are willing to significantly cut commissions in order to help sell your home.

For those people who are looking to sidestep Realtors, for sale by owner services, and discount brokerages have another option: the rent to own (RTO) option. You are working with buyers who do not qualify in the traditional sense to obtain a loan. These people rent the home from you for a period of time, typically three years, then obtain a mortgage and pay in full the remaining asking price of the home.

The idea of rent to own isn't new. It has been a part of real estate investing for years. Many people who enter the world of real estate investing like the aspect of RTO because they don't have to use their own money. I have been doing rent to own for years now, and not once have I had to invest my own money in the process. But, as with other things, there is a right and a wrong way to use this process to sell your home.

Unfortunately, there are too many "gurus" out there who are charging large amounts of money to teach people the RTO process. And, although the teachers do their best, many graduates of these investing courses are not ethical in their real estate investing practices.

That is why I wanted to start the *Rent to Own Revolution*. I wanted to pull back the curtain on the rent to own process. I wanted to show people that there is a right and wrong way to do this, and how you as a seller can understand that difference. I want to educate you so that you understand and can recognize good rent to own companies from the bad ones and avoid companies with less-than-ethical practices.

The Perfect Storm

From the movie "Perfect Storm"

Todd Gross, TV Meteorologist: Look, look at this. We got Hurricane Grace moving north off the Atlantic seaboard. Huge... getting massive. Two, this low south of Sable Island, ready to explode. Look at this. Three, a fresh cold front swooping down from Canada. But it's caught a ride on the jet stream... and is motoring hell-bent towards the Atlantic. What if Hurricane Grace runs smack into it? Add to the scenario this baby off Sable Island, scrounging for energy. She'll start feeding off both the Canadian cold front... and Hurricane Grace. You could be a meteorologist all your life... and never see something like this. It would be a disaster of epic proportions. It would be... the perfect storm.

That passage is from the George Cloony, Mark Wahlburg movie where they portray fishermen who head out to sea and end up in what is considered a "Perfect Storm", where all the independent conditions are merging at the same time and in the same place. A perfect storm is also brewing in the real estate industry, and there is a need for change and I have decided to be the catalyst for that change leading the way to what I'm calling the "Rent to Own Revolution".

In the past few years I have seen three different independent variables take a dramatic rise that individually would not be cause for change, but together has created the perfect environment for an individual like myself to take notice, step in and create a movement for change. Those three forces include:

- Increase in number of Tenant Buyers
- Increase in rent to own Investors
- Increase in number of Owners wanting to make more money on the sale of their home

Increase in the Number of Tenant Buyers

Before I start talking about why there is an increase in the number of tenant buyers it's important you know what is a Tenant Buyer. This is the name given to an individual who does not qualify for a traditional mortgage today and is seeking out or interested in getting into home ownership through a rent to own program. In later chapters I will get into the four different classifications and how to screen these individuals before you put them in your rent to own home.

Now don't get me wrong, there have always been people who for one reason or another don't qualify for a traditional mortgage. The majority of them aren't bad people, many of them just had a circumstance or two in their past that put some blemishes on their credit. Those can easily be fixed. But since 2008 after the financial crisis the federal government has made several changes to the rules for insured mortgages through the Canadian Mortgage and Housing Corporation (CMHC) and other private mortgage insurance providers like Genworth.

These rules will have the biggest impact on first time home buyers, however they affect everyone who buys a home with less than 20% down payment and those who are current homeowners looking to refinance their homes.

- The maximum amortization is back to 25 years, down from 40 years
- Home buyers can no longer get in with a zero down payment. 5% of the home purchase price is the minimum

- The maximum a homeowner can borrow against the equity in their home is 80%, down from 95%.
- The maximum gross debt service (GDS) ratio is 39% while the maximum total debt service (TDS) ratio is 44%. This becomes important in later chapters when we are screening Tenant Buyers for your rent to own home.
- The maximum amount of a line of credit a homeowner can have on their property is 65%, down from 80%

The biggest change that is affecting first time homebuyers is the length of mortgage decrease from 40 years down to 25 years. Although the interest rates did see record lows with people getting mortgages at just over 2%, people still had to qualify at a benchmark interest rate. At the time of writing, you can still get a mortgage just under 3% interest rate but must qualify at a rate of 5.24%. Obviously the banks are making sure the homeowners can afford the property should interest rates rise; however; with the increase in housing prices over time without a similar increase in salaries and wages, it is becoming increasingly difficult for people to get into home ownership.

While experts keep saying that income values will increase, their goals often seem to fall short of the real numbers. Even as recently as 2012, experts were saying that they were expecting salary rates to increase by 3.2%. Instead, the end of the year saw an average increase of only 2.8%. That is approximately equal to the increase for inflation rates in one month back in 2011. In November 2011, the inflation rate increased 2.9% while salaries only increased 2.7%, and in the next month only 1.4%.

When you are talking housing values, however, the gap increases even more. House values have risen over 100% since 2000, and approximately 50% since 2006. Those are fantastic numbers, but what do they mean? They mean many different things. One aspect of this increase is that the average home in Canada costs five times more than the average household income.

It can take up to 10 years for a person with a median income to save enough money for a down payment on even a modest home. In some parts of Canada, it costs as much as 80% of a household income to own and maintain a home.

That is a far cry from what finance experts used to say when discussing the ratio of family income to home ownership costs. It wasn't that long ago when experts were saying that a third of the family income should be designated for household expenses such as mortgage payments, maintenance, and repairs. Now these same experts are saying that almost half of the family income goes to expenses related to owning a home.

The homes in question aren't always elaborate mansions, but modest houses with little to no yard. While there has been an increase in the number of homes sold that are over $1 million, what a homeowner gets for that value has decreased.

Even Edmonton has seen a steady increase in home value, and income has not been able to keep up. Taking a look at this graph below, you'll be able to see all too clearly what I mean.

As you can see, house prices in Edmonton were always slightly higher than disposable incomes in the area. After 2005, however, the gap increased significantly between these two rates. This has led many people to believe that their dreams of home ownership will not be realized. Many people believed that after university they would be able to get a decent job, save some money, and after a few years buy a modest home. This hasn't happened for so many people, and many are beginning to believe it will take them 10 or 15 years in order to save the money they need to buy a house.

This discrepancy in income versus house value leaves homeowners in a bind at times as well. While more Canadians are willing to go into debt than was common several years ago, others are looking at home ownership as entering a phase of what has become known as house poor. What this means is that while these people own homes, and the value of the home continues to rise, their ability to afford the home comes into jeopardy. They are living paycheck to paycheck, or perhaps have the ability to stay 2 to 3 paychecks ahead of their expenses. This willingness to go into debt leaves people vulnerable if the housing rates continue on their present course or their mortgage payments increase beyond affordability.

Not only are some aspiring homeowners realizing that they have to change their idea of home ownership in terms of when they are able to buy a home, they also have to change the idea about what kind of home they can buy. They are starting to abandon their dreams of large backyards and of big homes where they can raise a large family. Now they are starting to believe that when they are finally at the point where they can buy a home, it will be very small and they'll be lucky if they have any yard at all for their future children to play in.

At the time of writing this book the government has stepped in and started making more changes. There is a great deal of downward pressure by the government to keep housing sales cool by restricting the amount of mortgages it guarantees under its

National Housing Act Mortgage-Backed Securities program. The finance minister has taken steps to cut the amount of credit to home buyers in fear the housing market could heat up amidst low interest rates.

As I stated earlier, there has always been tenant buyers, but you can see from the actions of the government and banks, as well as the substantial rise in housing prices and salaries not keeping pace, there are more and more individuals who are good people but just can't get qualified to buy a home today. Everything may be in order but because of the amount of homes the government will insure has decreased they may be just left out. As a result of all these factors there has been a dramatic increase in tenant buyers, especially in areas where rents are on the rise and vacancies are dropping.

Increase in Rent to Own Investors

I can still recall when I decided to get into real estate investing. It was 2008 and I was working as an independent business consultant and I had one major client, a sandblasting and painting company in Nisku Alberta. As a consultant I only got paid the hours I worked, so when I would take off for a sports trip with the guys around North America, not only would I be spending a couple thousand dollars but I would have lost my ability to make income while I was away. Doing what I was doing I couldn't leverage my time.

I then decided to look into how I could make money without having to work. Well, don't we all want the same thing? Make money and lie on the beach, travel the world, spend more time with family or whatever it is that makes you happy? It was then I started to open my eyes to the world around me, and how people were getting wealthy. It didn't take me long to discover many people took the road to riches via Real Estate.

One author in particular had received a great deal of attention and many of my friends and acquaintances had read his books and highly recommended I read the book Rich Dad, Poor Dad. The author, Robert Kiyosaki, had a series of books so I decided to buy 2-3 more in the series at that point in time to learn all I could about real estate investing.

I was on one of my many trips the last week of January and the first week of February 2009, this one through Europe for two weeks, when a good friend of mine Heather advised me there would be a free Rich Dad, Poor Dad two hour training session in Edmonton just after I returned to Edmonton. I asked her to enroll us both so we could check it out.

Going to the two hour seminar I had already known I wanted to get into real estate investing so whatever other training they were selling I was buying. I signed up for the three day weekend then at that event signed up for the Advanced Training courses along with coaching and mentoring, which ended up costing me close to $40,000.

Back then there weren't many companies coming around selling real estate investing training, but fast forward to today and it seems like there is a different company in every month. These companies are just churning out students, all being taught various strategies. As an avid networker I keep running into individuals each month that just finished a training program. Now I haven't been to all the programs, and spending large chucks of my money on high priced real estate education just isn't for me at the moment, but I have witnessed the massive increase in people doing rent to owns. Hell, most of them can't even be creative and just copy my ads word for word and just put their name and phone number in the ad.

This dramatic increase in individuals doing RTOs is going to gain more exposure for the industry. This exposure can both open up a larger market share for those who know how to do rent to owns and conduct them in an ethical and moral manner. Unfortunately it will also increase the number of unethical and shady investors who will cast a negative shadow on the industry, causing everyone to get painted with the same brush. My fear is the exposure is going to be negative and at the time of writing this book that fear has come true.

At the time of writing this book there was a report of a company operating out of Ontario that is being sued to the tune of $2 Million for defrauding homeowners, tenant buyers and investors alike. A scandal to this magnitude is what I feared, but only adds fire to my passion to start this revolution and expose the industry by pulling back the curtains for all to see how rent to own works and how people can make a substantial amount of money with them, while still operating with ethics and morality.

In Chapter 2 I will get into more detail about the increase in people being trained, but for now just know this is one of the three factors that is leading to the revolution.

Homeowners Wanting to Keep More Money

Since the market crash of 2007 there has been another substantial shift taking place. I witnessed it first hand when I first started to get into real estate investing and was focused on RTOs. Homeowners would call on my ad because they couldn't sell their home without incurring a substantial $20,000-40,000 payout penalty along with paying Realtor commissions.

Prior to the crash you had so many people buying homes and locking in their interest rates for 3-5 years. When the crash happened and people needed out of their homes they were faced with paying huge penalties to get out of their mortgage. Not only that but they were faced with paying real estate commissions to sell their homes.

Homeowners were searching for an alternative to selling their home, and the idea of renting their home for three years giving me the option to buy their home seemed like an ideal scenario. Unfortunately the market had dropped so significantly at the beginning that even with some modest appreciation the home still would not be worth what they owed. The only thing that was going to fix their situation was time. The homeowner needs time for the market to shift upwards, and for the principle of the mortgage to get paid down to the point where the value of the home is equal to the amount owing on the home.

It is now 2013 and since the crash of 2007 there has been little to no appreciation for the most part on the housing market in Edmonton. There are some pockets that may have gone up but most of the single-family homes have not appreciated, while townhouses and condos have taken the biggest hit, still not worth what they were in the peak.

I'm sure you will find similar scenarios in most markets of Canada. Some areas may have seen some modest appreciation, others being stagnant and some have yet to recover to the point they rose to in the peak of 2007.

As a result more and more people selling their homes are extremely conscious of the amount of equity they had in their home and how much they would get to keep when selling their home.

Over the past few years, especially since the market crash in 2007, people have become much more conscious of how much of their equity they be giving away to a Realtor just to sell their home that they started seeking alternative solutions.

Since that time, and as a result of the dramatic increase of people doing their own research for properties on line, more and more people have started using discount brokerages and for sale by owner systems to sell their homes. Many of these services can run anywhere from $500-$1,500 depending on the package you chose, but end up saving $10,000-$20,000 of your hard earned equity.

When the prices of the homes dropped in the late 2000's and people needed to sell and get out of their homes they found they couldn't afford to use a Realtor, otherwise they would end up paying the commissions out of their pocket. There was just not enough money to cover paying out the mortgage, penalties and paying the Realtor. During this time people started to analyze what their Realtor actually did for them and the price they were paying.

This can explain why, as the authors of *Freakonomics* put it, "most real-estate agents seem to spend 95 per cent of their energy chasing clients (for which they are paid nothing) and five per cent actually serving them (for which they are paid way too much)."

http://www.cbc.ca/news/canada/story/2010/02/11/f-vp-keller.html

I want to be clear; I am making some very general statements here. In no way could I operate my business without the help of my trusted Realtors to get me access to information that has not yet been released to the general public. I do, however, think that if the Competition Bureau opens up the MLS system completely, so the information is accessible to all, then the role of the Realtor will change substantially and may even go the route of the Travel Agent. That is just my personal opinion and right or wrong we are all entitled to them.

The internet has opened up the world, and more and more information is available on line, homeowners like yourself have the ability to get your home in front of just as many eyes looking for a home as your Realtor does. Many of the for sale by owner services and discount brokerages offer you the ability to post your home on the MLS system without paying the large broker fees and commissions when you sell your home.

This shift has spurned the growth of for sale by owner companies like ComFree and The Property Guys as well as discount brokerages. More and more homeowners like yourself want to keep as much of their hard earned equity as possible.

I'm sure you can already see the storm being created just from reading the last few pages. Homeowners want to make more money on their homes and give away less of their equity. An increase in the number of people looking to get into a rent to own and an increase in the exposure of rent to owns as a result of the increase in real estate investing training. It is all coming together.

After seeing all of the signs, I felt now is the time! Now is the time for me to stand up and lead a *Rent to Own Revolution*. A revolution that is built on ethics, integrity, and truly wanting to help others get more for their home while at the same time helping someone get into home ownership.

Rent to Own Revolution

The Revolution

revolution [ˌrɛvəˈluːʃən]

n

3. a far-reaching and drastic change, esp in ideas, methods, etc.

According to the Free Dictionary at the free dictionary.com, the definition a revolution is a far-reaching and drastic change, especially in ideas, methods etc. One famous past revolution where this was definitely the case was the Industrial Revolution.

It was a major turning point in history that transformed many human life circumstances. There were new ideas, new ways and methods of doing things and a drastic way in which we worked and lived. Some of those innovations included textiles, steam power and iron founding. There were also things like the development of the middle class, child labor, poor working conditions and the onset of the organization of labor.

During this time there was a massive transfer of knowledge, which is how the "Rent to own Revolution" will be developed. Throughout this book I aim to transfer my knowledge of rent to owns and the industry, which will expose the rent to own industry and pull back the curtains for all to see exactly how the strategy works, where the money is to be made, and what risks are involved so you will be able to recognize a legitimate operation from one operated by a less than ethical investor.

I am writing this book specifically for the Homeowners who:

- Want to make up to $60,000 or more extra from your home over the next three years then if you just sold today or turned it into a rental
- Want to get equity out of their home now and make money on their home for three years
- Don't want to deal with traditional tenants and the issues that come with having a rental property
- Want to reduce the amount of expenses your investment costs you
- Want to have a proven, reputable process and system for turning their home into a rent to own

This book is also for the Tenant Buyer who:

- Wants to know how rent to own works
- Wants to know how to determine, and what questions to ask to determine, if a rent to own company operates ethically.

And lastly, this book is for the Real Estate Investor who is:

- Looking to understand rent to own
- Evaluating if rent to own is a strategy they want to add to their portfolio
- Looking for a proven and reputable process and system for operating a Rent to own Company.

Just like In the Star Trek episode "Mirror, Mirror" there is a famous line that Captain Kirk says to First Officer Spock: "In every revolution, there is one man with a vision."

I also believe that this revolution needs someone with vision. A thought leader who has the expertise and the willingness to teach what they have learned to others. That is the purpose of this book. I want to teach you all that I know about the housing market, real estate investing, and the rent to own process. I want to be able to empower you with knowledge so that you can make an informed decision about the rent to own process. If you decide to use this process to sell your own home, you will be equipped with the necessary information and tools to do this the right way and to make a significant income in the process.

As you are reading through this book and my vision for the *Rent to own Revolution* ask yourself, "When am I going to join the Revolution?" Where do you want to be when the storm hits and the revolution starts? Do you want to be poised to take advantage of the situation and benefit or do you want to continue doing what you have always done because it is comfortable and what you know?

Opportunity

"A good hockey player plays where the puck is. A great hockey player plays where the puck is going to be."— Wayne Gretzky

The quote by Wayne Gretzky can equally be referenced in many businesses, especially in the real estate investing world and even more so when the Perfect Storm is about to hit and a *Rent to Own Revolution* is about to begin.

You can see it coming; I'm going to lead you and the rest of the revolutionaries to where the money is and how you can get it ethically and morally. This book is about the revolution that needs to take place, but also about educating you to be ready to take advantage and prosper from the opportunities that are available.

Throughout this book, I'm going to address the pains, fears and frustrations you may have with selling or renting your home, as well as entering into a rent to own agreement. I will go through five reasons you should turn your home into a rent to own and how you can make up to an extra $60,000 by doing so. I will also walk you through the steps you need to go through to ensure that you have a successful rent to own. I will discuss the importance of contracts and documentation.

ADDED BONUS

Access to a FREE Video Training program that discusses the 5 reasons to turn your home into a Rent To Own and how to calculate the amount of money you can make by turning your home into a Rent To Own. A $497 value absolutely free just by e-mailing your Amazon Receipt to receipts@RentToOwnRevolution.com.

Chapter 2

RIDING THE TRAINING WAVE

"When morality comes up against profit, it is seldom that profit loses."
— Shirley Chisholm

As I touched on in the previous chapter, I was working as a business consultant and had one major client when I came to the decision that I should get into real estate investing. It was a local company making about $1.5 million per year at the time and sometimes struggled to make payroll in the off-season. Within four short years I helped grow the company to $7 million in revenue by implementing processes, procedures, technology and assisting in the selection of key personnel.

During this time, the processes and procedures enabled the company to have a much healthier bottom line, which facilitated the ability to purchase land and build their own custom, state-of-the-art facility. As I was helping the company realize its full potential, it was normal to work 50-60 hours a week and 80 hours during busy times was not out of the norm.

I was also living a great life at the same time; I paid off all my debt during this time. Prior to investing in the education courses, I would treat my friends when we went out, I was riding in style with a fully loaded H3 and I would take off with my brother, Todd, cousin, Dean and friend, Jeff, a few times a year on some epic sports trips across North America. We would go to places like New York to catch a Yankees game, Rangers game and a Jets game all in four days. Throw in some site-seeing and we had an action-packed long weekend!

Oh how I loved our trips together, but I also enjoyed the weeklong all-inclusive holidays as well. Regardless of what kind of vacation I took, it was a double whammy on my finances. That was because, not only did it cost me money, but I was also unable to make any money during the time I was away. There is no leverage in the type of hands-on consulting such as what I was offering to my client.

Needless to say, I was enjoying life during my time consulting for the company. As much as I enjoyed the building process, and of course the money, I am an entrepreneur at heart and I was still trading time for money. That was when I realized two things. First, this gig wouldn't last forever so I needed to have a plan B. Second, plan B better have methods where I can still get paid as I travelled the world living life to the fullest!

It was late in 2008 when I started to look at ways where I could make money passively while I was living life traveling the world. Don't get me wrong, I wasn't looking to pack it all in the next day, but I was searching for something I could do while I was working my consulting job. I started to research how people got wealthy, and although there were lots of dot com billionaires, overnight Internet billionaires and people who built successful businesses leveraging the time, money and abilities of others, the majority of people over time gained their wealth through real estate.

I was quickly shown how real estate was one of the few things in the world where you could leverage your money. You could buy a place worth $250,000 with only $12,500 at the time and the bank would cover the rest. Wow, I remember thinking this is the way to go...I could buy properties then rent them out and make money each and every month. So I started doing some more research and buying some books to read. I ended up buying 3-4 books from a popular series on real estate investing prior to a 2-week trip I was about to take to Germany, France and Spain. There was going to be lots of travel days on the train between destinations, so I wanted to have some books to go through during that time.

It was the last week of January and the first week of February that I had arranged time off so I could head to Europe with my friends, Jeff and Corrine. It wasn't the best time of year to be going to these places but it was a slow season where I was working, as it was for Jeff at Canadian Tire. Corrine worked for the government, so I don't think it really mattered when she took holidays. We decided to fly into Frankfurt because the flight was quite a bit cheaper than to Paris. Also, it was the first time any of us had been to Europe, so we wanted to see as much of it as we could. We had one week to see a few cities before we had to be in Malaga, Spain for the final week. I used the owners of the sandblasting and painting company's timeshare to book a week at a complex just outside Malaga.

I don't recall exactly where I was at the time, but during the two weeks in Europe I received either a text message or an email from my good friend, Heather, advising me that the author of the Rich Dad, Poor Dad series I was reading was offering a free two hour seminar in Edmonton just shortly after I returned, and wanted to know if she should sign me up. I immediately said yes, as I knew I wanted to learn more.

Now back in Edmonton, it was the night of the free two hour event. I had already known I was going to get into real estate investing and was willing to take some courses to speed up the learning curve, so if there was more training offered I knew I was going to get involved. I had been to enough workshops and training programs with the various companies I worked for that I was expecting a sales pitch. Yup, there it was a three-day training program for $500 and I get to bring a guest for free. I am positive I was the first one to sign up with Heather as my free guest. I was set; I was going to fast track my education so I knew how to do real estate investing the right way.

The next month the company was back for the three day weekend event and I was stoked! I still remember the people, one of them was the presenter and he was from the United States. The presenter was great, that U.S. accent of his and his teaching style kept our attention. You could tell this guy could sell. Early on at the event, he got us to write down a couple of numbers and made the comment that if you were serious about being a real estate investor you could expect to pay around $12,000-$40,000. Now he didn't come out and say it, but in the back of my mind I knew that there was going to be a sales pitch and the cost of the programs were going to be somewhere in the neighborhood of $12,000-$40,000.

During the first day, the presenter talked about financing deals and how people could do it with what they had available. He talked about RRSPs, equity, lines of credit and even credit cards. When he came to credit cards, he showed people strategies of how to use the funds in deals and how, by having access to enough of a limit on a couple of cards, you could use the money quite cheaply. He then encouraged everyone to call the credit card companies and request better interest rates, better terms, reducing the yearly fee and raising the limits. This all came together at the end of the event when it was time to present to courses and the prices.

As I had thought early on, the courses ranged from $12,000-$40,000 depending on how many you purchased and if you had a mentor or not. I talked it over with Heather and informed her that I was taking some of the classes and I also was taking advantage of the mentoring. I suggested that if she wanted to come we could split the cost. She agreed and we paid $32,000 total, so each ended up paying $16,000. This was after we had contacted our credit card companies and raised our limits, so we used these same cards to cover the cost of the courses.

See, there was an underlying motive to getting us to raise the credit card limits.

That was it, we signed up and we were enrolled. We would be sent our course material and a list of courses. I received a call within a week or two by a company rep who talked me into paying another $8,000 for phone coaching. They were talking about how they could help kick start things, etc., etc., blah, blah, blah...well I bought it, and what a waste of time that was. I was so self-motivated that I was already way past what the coach was talking about. The only real value I received from the coach is he inadvertently gave me the idea for my real estate investing company name, which was how the name ioffersolutions Real Estate Services, Inc. came to be.

Time was going by quickly. The 3-day event was in March and we had booked three courses to take between April and June. Each course was 3 days long and we had to travel to get to the courses. Two were being held in Vancouver and one in Calgary. The first course taught us about analyzing properties for buy, rent and hold strategies. It also touched on some of the other courses we would be taking later such as buy, fix and sell, creative finance and lease option (rent to own). The second course we took was on creative finance and the third one was lease option, which was held in the beginning of June.

It was during the lease option course that I had decided this was the strategy I was going to focus on. It was a true, no money down strategy when you did what was called a sandwich lease option. This is where I lease the home from a homeowner with the option to buy in the future, then turn around and find someone looking to get into a home that doesn't qualify for a mortgage today, get into that home and sub-lease it to them and give them the option to buy the home in the future. Wow, it was genius!

The instructor, who ended up being my mentor, was actually the guy (who I had come to find out) wrote the manuals for most of the courses. He was the guy who built the training company years ago to be the fulfillment organization for companies like the one that did the marketing and selling of the courses that I attended. He had been an investor since the 80s, and was an unassuming farmer from Okatoks, Alberta, but was a genius. He would come across as a simple farmer but it was all part of his negotiating technique and this guy could get people interested in turning their homes into a RTO. He would do calls in front of the class to set up meetings with homeowners and with a simple script had the homeowners willing to meet and have a discussion about turning their home into a rent to own. He booked the meetings for the students to go and meet the people.

That was it, I knew that the sandwich lease option was the way I was going to go and what I was going to focus on. I had just racked up $24,000 on my credit cards for training and coaching, but knew with my job that I could have that paid off within 6-9 months. And that's when it happened. On June 29, just a couple of weeks after the rent to own training course, the owners of the sandblasting and painting company came to me and told me tomorrow was my last day.

You see, as a result of the recession initiated by the housing crisis in the U.S. and the drop in the price of oil and natural gas, which drives much of the Alberta economy and definitely affects the oil companies (clients of the sand blasting and painting company), work at the shops had come to a standstill. We were already down to a skeleton crew, and having a high-priced consultant around who actually doesn't contribute to the work that generates income just didn't make for good business sense. One of the many things the owners learned over my four years there was to make business decisions on what was the best for the company; instead of keeping people around because of some sense of loyalty they felt towards the people.

So that was it, I packed up my office on June 30 and my mood was quite down. I'm not going to say I was depressed, because that is a clinical term, but I was scared of the unknown and the future. I knew I had enough cash in the bank to last me for 3 months. I spent a lot of time deliberating about if I was going to try and find another contract in this recession, try to get a job or take my newly acquired real estate investing training and start my new venture in the world of rent to own. Well, the decision was made; real estate investing it was going to be and rent to own was to be the strategy. The next day, July 1, 2009 was the beginning of my new venture.

July 1, 2009 — The Start of My Rent to Own Business (Ok, July 2 because July 1 was a holiday)

Back in March, when I was doing my weekly phone coaching, I had created a Hotmail account specifically for real estate investing. When I was discussing the address with my coach, the address was ibuyproblems@hotmail.com. He indicated that it had a negative connotation and that I should try for something more positive. He started rhyming off positive groups of words together for me to use as an email address then all of a sudden he said it, "I Offer Solutions." That was it, as soon as the words were out of his mouth I did a domain search for ioffersolutions.com and ioffersolutions.ca and they were both available. Before we got off that call, I had bought both website domain names and was doing a Canadian corporate search on the name as well. Low and behold, it was available so I federally registered the name to be used in every province in the country. That is how the company name ioffersolutions Real Estate Services, Inc. came to existence.

As soon as I had the domains registered in March, I knew it was time to build the websites. Since I had previously had websites for an online nutritional consulting and personal training business that I shut down as a result of partner differences, I had learned quite a bit about websites and attracting people to your sites by researching what people were looking for and making sure I positioned myself to be where they were looking. Now I'm no techie or coder, but I was using a system at the time that enabled me to upload, and drag and drop into templates that made building websites easy. I also knew the strategies to get my website found quickly when people were searching the Internet for specific topics.

I started to build the site and in a matter of days it was complete. I had done everything I had learned to get my site ranked high in the search engines based on the content I put in the site. Fast forward to July, when it was time I took this business up a notch and was already on the first page of Google for the term rent to own in Edmonton. I was also ranking high for the phrases "stop foreclosure" and "avoid foreclosure." This was perfect, and I had already been getting some calls and emails prior to July from the website, but nothing I could act on.

Prior to July, I had business cards made up. I grabbed a logo of a house in a hand from the Internet and using VistaPrint.ca and I got cards made up and sent to me for just the cost of shipping. Having the website along with the business cards and a business name made me appear to be a much more credible real estate investing company than the novice beginner I was. Fortunately, I had experience starting a business from scratch and had just spent the last four years helping someone else build his company, so I had an idea what I was doing. Now, I just needed to get some homeowners to agree to lease option their house to me.

During the RTO course in June, the trainer had given us the script he used to cold call people to get them to meet with you about renting to own their home. There was just one thing about it I didn't like and that was the homeowner thought you were a potential tenant and not a real estate investor. I had a problem with that, not to mention the fact that I didn't like the idea of picking up the phone and cold calling people. That was so far out of my comfort zone that I just couldn't bring myself to do it. I had to come up with a better alternative.

Since I had done quite a bit of Internet work to research the competition in Edmonton, I had come across the website Kijiji. I can't recall if I actually knew of the website prior to July 2009 but I know it is when I kicked things into gear. Since I wasn't the type to call homeowners, I figured I would have them call me. I also wanted them to know exactly what I wanted so that when they called, I wouldn't have to try very hard to get a meeting. When someone calls me I'm in the position of power, so I have a completely different mindset than if I call someone. That is when I came up with the one ad that has brought me more phone calls than all my other ads combined.

Here is the image I used in conjunction with the ad on the following page:

HEADLINE OF AD: COMPANY NEEDS 8 HOMES FOR OCT 1 TO RENT 2-3 YRS THEN BUY

BODY OF AD
Local Investment Company looking to rent houses, town homes, condos, duplexes for 2-3 years then purchase the properties at the end of the lease. We require properties in Edmonton and surrounding areas such as Sherwood Park, Spruce Grove, Leduc, St. Albert, Stony Plain, etc.

Company has clients looking to relocate to the areas listed above.

OUR COMPANY DOES THE FOLLOWING:
-Pays your rent by the 15th of every month GUARANTEED!
-Puts quality tenants into your property

-Provides a long-term lease agreement (from 1-5 years)
-Handles all the management responsibilities
-Handles all the maintenance and repairs up to $500 per instance
-Provides interior insurance
-Buys your house at the end of the lease term at a GUARANTEED price
-Closes quickly

For more information please contact JOHN at our office

ioffersolutions Real Estate Services, Inc.
Suite 126, 9768 170 Street
Edmonton, Ab
Call John 780-XXX_XXXX
http://www.ioffersolutions.com

That ad is so successful that I only change the month in the headline each month. It has been copied word for word, or the concept has been copied by other real estate investors in Edmonton and other cities looking to sandwich lease homes to turn them into rent to owns.

Well, the very first day I posted that ad the phone started ringing. I would typically post the ad two times a day. I would have to delete the ad then repost it in order for it to stay on the first five pages. I think in the first week I had at least five homeowners willing to meet with me about my company renting their home for 2-3 years and then buying the home.

Churning out the Investors

Doing all my Google searching and research when I started full time into rent to own, I had discovered there were really only three companies that I could find that had any exposure at all on the Internet. Of those three, there were only two that advertised on Kijiji. Now when I search for rent to own homes Edmonton there are five companies on the first page of Google alone. Fortunately, I hold three different positions on that first page and four more positions on page two. But the deeper you go in the Google pages; you will end up finding another 5-10 companies advertising to do RTOs in the Edmonton and surrounding area.

Now those are just the people who have actually made it to the first five pages of Google, there are so many more who have websites and not even made it that far as of yet. If I were to go to Kijiji, I would probably find double the number of people trying to get people to contact them who don't qualify for a traditional mortgage today or who are looking for homeowners to lease their homes to them, giving them the option to buy. As mentioned previously, many have taken my "Gold Mine" ad and duplicated it in full or part to get homeowners to contact them.

There are real estate training companies coming through almost monthly pitching their training programs, educating and convincing people that it is so easy to do "No money down" real estate. I would hazard a guess that there are approximately 300-500 individuals per year in Edmonton alone being taught various real estate investing techniques. I have been to almost all of the free events, watched the number of people who signed up for the 3-day weekends and spoke to various individuals who went on to take the training, to discuss how many people went through with the full training. The real estate training business is a very lucrative business, or at least it used to be. The enrollment has decreased over the past year or two but they are still churning them out.

As a successful investor and avid networker, people who want to meet me for coffee contact me on a regular basis. I love meeting people, but it gets to be the same old, same old when I meet these new investors who are all hopped up on hopes and dreams only to quit or get beaten down when reality sets in as to how hard it is to actually make a living doing no money down real estate. As my wise mentor told me, it is "consistent persistent" that gets you to where you want to be. That and focusing on one specific thing while being open and educated when other opportunities come your way. As he puts it, you do rent to own, rent to own, rent to own, a foreclosure, rent to own, rent to own, a buy-fix-sell, rent to own, rent to own, etc. You get the idea.

Once people realize that doing this once a week for a couple of hours doesn't get them the vast riches they were expecting, or realize just how much work they would have to put in to make it work, most of them quit and say, "Well I tried that real estate investing thing, it doesn't really work." That is why when new people contact me to meet up for coffee I tell them the reality of the situation, whether they want to hear it or not. This no money down business is a lot of work, and to be successful, you need to work it consistently on a persistent basis. Basically, I live, breathe and eat RTOs. Meeting with homeowners, talking on the phone with tenant buyers, processing applications, posting ads, website and SEO work...I work more now then when I had an actual job. My success comes from how much time I put in. Fortunately, my early work with the Internet has saved me some time because my website gets a lot of visitors, and I have a lot of information available to everyone.

I'm sorry if I'm a dream smasher, but I like to be a realist when I talk to these people. I have coached and mentored over a dozen investors in the Edmonton area, many of which are my direct competition in the rent to own business. I get asked regularly to mentor others who are interested in learning how to do real estate investing. It has gotten to the point where I don't want to take money from people who can't commit to doing this business.

I am upfront and honest. I tell people: "If you can't commit to doing this business every day for at least 1-2 hours then I don't want to take your money. You will end up paying me. I will take you to meetings so you can see firsthand how to actually do this business. I hate classroom style; I'm all about the field trips and actual hands on work. And after our four weeks are up, you will realize that you just paid me to show you things that you will probably never do. Then I feel bad for taking your money and that isn't a feeling I like to have."

When talking to people who want to pay me a couple of thousand dollars for one month of coaching, you might think that I am insane to convince them not to hire me and to turn away the "free" money. I do it this way because I only want to help those who are serious about this business, or have access to money. If you have access to money, then you don't need to work as hard to find opportunities because others will find them for you. People who have access to money and credit will have their pick of investment opportunities so for them I just need to help them understand the strategies and importance of networking. I help them determine what their strategies are going to be, how to analyze the opportunities and set goals and benchmarks that the deals must meet, and how to be prepared with multiple exit strategies. If people want to focus on no money down real estate then they must be willing to commit to consistent persistence.

Many People Use this Training in an Unethical Manner

Now as a result of all this education and training you get people with all different kinds of ethics and morals working in this business, which is unfortunate. This is an industry that is not regulated by any governing body, like real estate sales or the landlord and tenant act. The courts govern it and things can really get messy, especially when you don't have your documentation in order or you are taking advantage of others. This is truly where renting to own gets a bad name. Most people think that just because they have a signed contract they are going to win in court, that isn't always the case.

If the judge thinks you have taken advantage of the person, not educated them into what they are getting into, they didn't understand the contracts, or the contracts are unreasonable, then you can just as easily lose your "slam-dunk" case.

When you get an abundance of people being trained to do these no money down deals or rent to owns, you are bound to get a great deal of people who operate in a less than moral or ethical way. This has always been something I have been against. I have a very good moral and ethical compass, I usually try to do the right thing or what is best for all people involved. This was the main reason why I created a process for pre-qualifying individuals to get into the rent to own homes about a year after I started my rent to own business.

When I first started out and needed people to get into the homes, I based their qualifications on whether they had the down payment required, could afford the monthly payment and had good references. I did go through the contracts as I was taught — the inspection of the home, advising the tenant buyer to seek legal advice and so on, but I knew there was more I could do.

Through my networking, I had met a mortgage broker and a credit coach that I had just clicked with, and together we worked out a process to ensure that we were doing everything possible for people looking to get into a rent to own. We then went to work and created a very specific process that the individuals must go through before we consider them for our program. We standardized the documentation; we laid out a specific process of what happens when the application comes in and where it goes next. The process worked so well that we rolled it out to the individuals I was coaching and mentoring to do this business. Soon, every real estate investor I dealt with was using the exact same documentation. They were also using the same mortgage brokerage and credit coach to process the tenant buyers looking to get into a rent to own home.

I had standardized the entire RTO process for any and all investors who were associated with my company and me, but I knew that was only part of the process. You see, it was easy to set myself apart from every other rent to own company before, because of my process and I just knew I would always do the right thing, but the bottom line is this is still a business and as long as people know exactly what they are getting themselves into at the beginning, then it becomes about business.

I know there are still lots of people operating their rent to own companies with no regard for the people they put in the homes. They do it to take the person's down payment money, take the monthly rent and make cash flow on that. They give the people an unrealistic short timeframe to qualify such as 12-18 months, but never know if the people will ever qualify for the home at the end. Another thing these shady investors will do is not change the contract price at the end of the rent to own period.

When a person gets into a rent to own, typically they agree to purchase the home in the future so the purchase price is an appreciated value. It is all-good if the home gets to that value but in the last four years in Edmonton, there has been little to no appreciation. So anyone that has been in a rent to own during that time will undoubtedly be faced with buying a home that is overpriced. Now this is where you separate the shady investors who are in it just for the money with the investors who are willing to do what is right.

I'm going to give you my exact example and explain what a shady investor would do, then explain what I did in this situation. The home was in Sherwood Park and I had an agreement with Joe and Julie (not their real names), the owners, to lease their home for three years with the option to buy the home at the end of the three years. Mark and Evette (not their real names) were the tenant buyers who were going to buy the home at the end of the three years. At the time I signed the home with the homeowners, it was worth approximately $320,000 and I had an agreement to buy it from them for $291,500, which would have been approximately what they would have received if they sold it through traditional real estate methods.

Using the $320,000 as the base, I calculated the end price of the home to be $379,000 in three years. Looking at this now, which was the 2nd deal I ever did, the appreciated value was way too aggressive. Well, six months prior to the end of the three years, I had Mark send all his information to the mortgage broker to make sure the broker was going to ok the purchase of the home. It came back that Mark had a cell phone collection on his record recently. Come to find out, Mark broke his contract and switched providers and said he paid the contract out after a fight with the company, but they claim he didn't. Regardless, it was on his credit bureau report. Based on this information, the broker said there is no way he was getting qualified until it was resolved.

Mark spent a couple of months getting things resolved but we were very close to the purchase date and the mortgage broker advised that she couldn't get Mark qualified because not enough time had passed and we needed at least six more months. At this point, a shady investor would tell Mark that because he can't qualify for the home he would have to leave the home at the end of his lease, and by the way, the non-refundable option is just that, non-refundable.

Now, because my contract with Joe and Sandy had an automatic three month renewal, which I have since changed to twelve months just for situations like this, I knew all I had to do was convince Joe and Julie to give me another three months and Mark would be in great shape. I got them to agree, which cost me an additional $1,500 on the purchase price with Joe and Julie, which also means that I'm now up to $293,000 for the purchase, but I've done something good for Mark and Evette so I'm happy.

So we go five months into the six month extension and I get Mark and Evette to contact the mortgage broker again to see about qualifying for the home and they are approved by an "A" lender, which would be like one of the big five banks. However, none of the government insurers would insure the mortgage. You see, Mark had built up 5% so the mortgage had to be insured by CMHC, Genworth, etc. There is no way they would insure the mortgage because the collection was still too fresh. They advised it would be another 6-12 months. Wow, what a devastating blow.

It took a lot of convincing to get Joe and Julie to extend. I knew they weren't going to extend again so I was faced with trying to get an investor involved to buy the home from Joe and Julie at my price then continue on with the rent to own. Meanwhile, my mortgage broker was working some ninja moves of her own with lenders and managed to find Mark some financing though a "B" lender, which means higher interest rates and they side step the insurer by a combination of more cash down and other mortgages.

Now, I might lose some of you here, but I'm going to do my best to explain the numbers and how this all played out. If you remember, I had an agreement with Mark for him to buy the place for $379,000. Well, when the house was appraised by the lender it came back at $325,000. Wow, it only went up by $5,000 in the 3.5 years. Ok, so here again is what a shady investor would do; they would tell Mark and Evette that they would have to come up with the shortfall, the difference between the $379,000 and the $325,000 in cash in order to buy this house. Another thing the investor would do is take some of it in cash and the rest they would register in a promissory note or mortgage on the property for the remaining value, that way there was a good chance they would end up taking the property back.

Now in Mark's case he paid $10,000 down upfront and I credited an additional $300 per month every time the rent was paid on time and in full. So for 42 months, they would have had 42 times $300, so an additional $12,600 would be used as their down payment. So based on the purchase of $379,000, they would have had $22,600 for a down payment. However, the home wasn't worth $379,000, it was only worth $325,000. So now I had to figure out what to do to make this sale happen and hope to make at least $5,000 I needed to cover legal costs, accounting costs and company costs.

I looked at the appraised price of $325,000 and figured out that if I just credited Mark the 5% necessary then that would leave me with $308,750, which still made sense since my purchase price with Joe and Julie was $293,000. I felt good; things were coming together until I got a call from the mortgage broker. She then advised me that in order for Mark to get the mortgage through the "B" lender, who doesn't recognize rent credits and won't allow a simultaneous close, I needed to structure the sale of the home directly from Joe and Julie to Mark and Evette. I'll get into that more in a bit, but first let's look at what had to take place in order for this sale to go through.

If you recall the rent credits was the $300 each month I credited Mark when he paid his rent on time. This particular lender won't allow Mark to use these towards his down payment, which meant on the $325,000 purchase Mark only had $10,000 down. Now this had nothing to do with the RTO contracts, me, the mortgage broker, or Mark, but the "B" lender. If Mark had been approved with an "A" lender, they would have recognized the credits, but since the lenders make their own rules, this lender would not allow them.

The "B" lender agreed to give Mark the following:
1st mortgage - $243,750.00
2nd mortgage - $32,500.00

This made a total of $276,000, plus adds in Mark's initial $10,000 payment when he got into the rent to own and he was up to $286,000. That left a difference of $325,000 -$286,000 = $39,000 for Mark to come up with just to buy the home at its current value.

If you think you are getting tired and confused, imagine how I felt on this roller coaster. When most shady investors would have just told them too bad, so sad, here I am doing anything and everything to get them into home ownership. I talked with my mortgage broker again, as she was dealing with Mark and Evette as well as the lenders, and she told me the lender would accept a VTB (Vender Take Back) from the seller up to a value of $16,000.

For those of you who don't know, a VTB is when the owner of the home agrees to forego some of the cash proceeds from the sale in exchange for placing a mortgage on the home. In this case $16,000 of the proceeds of the sale would be in the form of a Mortgage the owner would have registered on the house. Even though I was structuring this deal between the owner and the tenant directly, this $16,000 was to come from my share of the proceeds.

Now if you recall, I had a deal to pay the owners $293,000 for the home so I had to make sure they received that money at the sale. This meant the total of the first mortgage, second mortgage, plus cash had to at least be that much; otherwise, I'm paying out of my pocket to make this sale happen.

Now, with this new information let's see where we are at:

1st mortgage:	$243,750.00
2nd mortgage:	$32,500.00
Total	$276,250.00

This represents cash to owner as well

Initial rent to own payment:	$10,000
VTB (from me)	$16,000
Total	$26,000

Total so far:	$276,250
	$ 26,000
	$302,250
Minus total needed	$325,000
Short	$ 22,750

As we stood at this point, Mark would have to come up with $22,750 cash in order to buy this house, otherwise he would end up losing the home.

As I stated so many times, we are only going through this because Mark couldn't get qualified by an "A" lender. Giving you an example of someone who qualifies wouldn't show you the lengths that investors like myself will go to help people in this business. I can guarantee you that the majority of people doing this business would have given up when Mark couldn't qualify, leaving nothing but a mess and potential court appearances to rectify.

So to wrap this story up, Mark did come up with the money to buy the home and in the end, even though he wasn't allowed to use the rent credits, I did the right thing by dropping the price to fair market value, which more than made up for the lost credits.

Just to let you know, this whole process took approximately 45 days after the initial close date, so in total I think we worked on this for at least 60 days. It was a rollercoaster ride to say the least. In the end, Mark ended up owning the home, the homeowner got what they wanted from the sale and I made $6,000 cash and a $16,000 mortgage against the property that Mark makes monthly payments on. All in all, everyone walked away winners.

Starting a Rent to Own Service

Going though that recent experience made me realize several things. First, very few people actually realize the lengths that I will go and the things I will do in order to do the right thing and help others. Being someone of service first came from my parents, Shirley and Wilson (Gary) McCabe. We grew up in a loving middle class family where our parents instilled good morals and ethics in me and my brothers Todd and Trevor. We had a somewhat strict upbringing but we always had the things we needed.

Much of our parents' disposable income went to putting us in organized hockey and fast pitch softball. Our parents where the type who always went to the games, always carpooled the other players, always volunteered to help with the fundraising, the fields, the organizing, whatever it took. It didn't stop with just us kids and our sports; they were they type of people who always gave their time and energy to help others and asked nothing in return. They are very proud people who have a hard time accepting help from others but are always the first ones to offer when it is needed.

Even though I am my own person, I give all the credit of my morality, ethics and treating others, as I myself would like to be treated, to my mom and dad. I thank them and I love them dearly.

Secondly, there were areas of the process that I went through with Mark, Evette, Joe and Julie that I needed to have more control over. I needed to change my contracts so that if the situation were to rise again, everyone would know exactly what would take place. The homeowners realize I will have a 12-month automatic extension that I can exercise to use if needed, the buyers will know exactly what happens should the home not appraise at the value in the contracts, and it will be spelled out what will happen to the rent credits or option payment should the lender not accept them.

Thirdly, after I make all these changes to my process, I need a vehicle to promote how a great rent to own company should operate, making the entire process transparent to all parties and educate everyone from homeowners to tenant buyers so they can spot shady investors. For all these reasons mentioned, I decided to create the rent to own service, write this book, teach people the rent to own process and offer a solution where investors can align themselves with the revolution so that they can be recognized for operating in an ethical and transparent manner. I would also provide them with a solid, sound and proven business model and process they can count on.

I know that not everyone who is in this business is going to treat people the way I do, and that there are also people who are trying to do RTO with no education or incomplete information at best.

You don't have to be unethical in order to make money. In my time running a rent to own service, I have never felt the need to resort to unethical business practices. On the contrary, I make every effort to make my business transparent and to make sure that everyone involved understands the process every step of the way. I believe in customer satisfaction and giving my clients the respect that they deserve. I make sure that sellers receive a fair asking price for their property and I don't try to drive down the value of the home in order to make a profit. I treat potential tenant buyers fairly and don't try to obtain additional money at the end of the agreement by telling the buyers that the appraised value is less and that they are responsible for the difference.

As with many different types of strategies, it is the scam artists and the people who do things illegally who end up with the most publicity. The people who are doing it right and make money in an ethical manner don't always receive the attention they deserve. That is why I want to talk to you about the right and wrong way to go about the rent to own process. I will show you ways that other people have sold their own home through rent to own and made a lot of money. I will also show you how I help people every day learn the best way to sell their home. By pulling back the curtain, I hope to shine a light on the whole process and to allow the good guys to receive decent exposure for once.

I understand that there are reasons why the rent to own process and real estate investing has such negative reputation and I feel that if I am going to legitimately lead the charge in the *Rent to Own Revolution* that I have to be able to be above reproach.

The true test of a man's character is the way he behaves when he thinks no one is looking. To me, taking advantage of buyers or sellers who are ignorant is like behaving improperly when no one is looking. My determination to create and maintain ethical practices in my business is one of the reasons why I have been so successful over the years. This is why I am willing to lay all of my cards on the table and explain this process to you in this book. By the time you are done reading this, you will not only understand the right way to sell your home through the rent to own process but also how to recognize companies that are using an ethical processes to obtain or sell homes via renting to own.

Chapter 3

WHAT OPTIONS DO HOMEOWNERS HAVE?

"There is no place more delightful than one's own fireplace."-- Marcus Tullius Cicero

"Home is a shelter from storms — all sorts of storms."-- William J. Bennett

"The light is what guides you home, the warmth is what keeps you there."-- Ellie Rodriguez

The above quotes show that home has always been an important concept and different cultures around the world value home ownership. Most of us put a lot of time and love into a home. When it comes time to sell it, for whatever reason, we can't let our ignorance and sentiment get in the way of making sure we are making the right choices. The first step in making the best choice is understanding all of the options that are available.

One of the biggest challenges in starting the Revolution is that the majority of people don't even realize it is an option. Every time a homeowner contacts me on my "Gold Mine" ad and I get into the explanation, the response is always the same: "I've never heard of a service like that before". Not that they haven't heard of rent to own, just that they haven't heard of a company that facilitates and offers a RTO service. That is mainly because it has been handled by small time investors who don't traditionally market the services to the masses. Instead, they approach homeowners who have their home for sale or rent and then offer them the option.

For that main reason, most homeowners are only aware of selling their home with a Realtor, selling their home privately or renting their home out, because they couldn't sell it at the time.

Once people become homeowners anything can happen that could cause them to need to get out of their home and either upsize, downsize, relocate or just move on to a new chapter in their life. When this happens the first thing that comes to the homeowner's mind is to sell their home, take what equity they have and start fresh somewhere else. This is primarily because that is what we have been trained to do or what the majority of people do, so how can all those people be wrong.

One of the many problems with today's society is the lack of financial education in the school system, specifically around real estate and wealth generation. As so many of us have heard Robert Kiyosaki say over and over, we are ingrained to go to school, get good grades and then get a good job. And this is just what people do and preach to their children. We are creating a nation of worker bees so the rich can keep getting richer and the middle class can stay just 1-2 paychecks above broke.

It is for that very reason the majority of people choose to sell their homes when they need to make a change. They require the money they have created in equity to move on, but then end up using any excess money to fund things like vacations, purchase travel trailers, quads, boats and other "toys." Many times they will finance these items, increasing their monthly debt load only to get themselves in trouble again down the road.

Selling My House

It was 2003, no more than a couple of years after buying my home that I had made the decision to go back to university and get my MBA. Before I could start my MBA, however, I needed to complete a few courses at Acadia University in Nova Scotia to complete my business degree. I had originally left university to take a full time job, where I was promoted and transferred to Edmonton in 1997.

In 2001 I had a major life changing event other than buying my home, and that was the fact that I lost 100 lbs. in six months. It was all with the help from some bodybuilders who taught nutritional consulting. They educated me in how eating affected your appearance and how by just making some minor changes to my nutrition and continuing doing what I was doing by playing sports and going to the gym daily, I would see results.

They were correct, the weight just flew off. Only a few months after I had lost all the weight I went on my first ever vacation with a couple of friends. I went to Puerto Vallarta Mexico. I was feeling good and looking good and had a simply amazing time. It was then my love for travel was born.

Having gone through this change there were a couple things I realized. First, I wanted to travel the world a lot more. Second, in order to have the money necessary to travel I needed to increase my earning potential, which meant finishing my degree and getting my MBA so I could become a business consultant. So that was it, in January of 2003 I had formulated my plan. That summer I needed to take six weeks off work to attend spring and summer sessions at university, taking four of the six courses that were remaining for my degree.

I was going to sell my home and use the money I made to help further my plans. I was going to remain at work until the following summer, getting the last two courses I needed through correspondence or at the U of A, and then register for my MBA after Christmas. In the summer, before going back to school, I planned on going on a Contiki tour for individuals under 35 for a month long trip. It was going to be great.

The plan was laid. The first thing I had to do was sell my house. To do that I knew I needed to make some changes and do some work to the home. It was ok for me, but after living there for a couple of years and I realized there were many things that needed to be changed to make it more appealing to a broader audience. Things like getting rid of the awful carpet on the main floor so that I could replace it with laminate flooring, get rid of the wood panel in the living room and give the entire main floor a paint makeover.

Also, new trim throughout the entire place was needed. Now I'm going to be the first to tell you, I'm no carpenter, but I did all the work myself. Some was good; some looked like it was done by someone who didn't know what he or she was doing.

Well, the home was finally done enough, and it was time to hit the spring market. It was still winter so the snow covered the roof shingles that needed to be replaced in a year or two. Well the house didn't sell before the snow melted so the roof detracted from the sale. Eventually a young couple came along and was interested in the home. Obviously there were some negotiations regarding the shingles and furnace. We came to an agreement and the house was sold. I did end up selling the home for slightly more than I paid for it, but when it came down to collecting my money when it was all said and done, I walked away with next to nothing.

If I had only known then what I know now. So, the 5% I put down on the house – gone, the pay down of the mortgage – gone, difference between buying and selling the home – gone.

Where did it all go you ask?

- Well, the bank charged me a penalty for selling into a locked in term of the mortgage – That cost me a couple of grand
- The Realtor walked away with about $8,200

- The lawyer took about $900-$1,000

When it was all said and done, I was lucky to get away without paying! I was determined to never go through that again.

Now I know how to capitalize on owning a home and I want to pass on what I have learned and been able to help other home owners just like you do since 2009.

Sell with a Realtor

This is the option almost everyone takes because it is what everyone does and most people aren't financially educated. I know that is the method I used for selling my first home because I didn't know any better. You would think that this is a simple process. You find a Realtor, they list the home, they show the home, they sell the home, and then you are able to pay off your mortgage. Depending on how long you have lived in that home and how far you pay down your equity, you may even be thinking that you will be able to have some money left over. Unfortunately; however, that is not the way it happens the majority of the time.

The first problem that you run into with selling with the Realtor is finding the right Realtor to list your home. Advertisements for Realtors are everywhere. You see them on TV, you see them in the real estate section of the paper, and you even see them on homes that are for sale. All of these Realtors seem to be promising you the same thing. They are telling you that if you list with them they will be able to sell your home for you quickly and at a great price.

How do you go about finding a good Realtor? You may ask friends and family for recommendations or you may visit a few real estate offices and listen to the sales pitch. That is exactly what it is that they are offering you. They want your listing because that is how they make their money. Most of these Realtors are very good at selling. This means they also know how to read people. It doesn't take long for a good real estate agent to read your body language and understand exactly what it is that they need to tell you in order to obtain your listing.

Many of these excellent real estate agents worked their way to the top and now have an office with several real estate agents underneath them. They are the face of the company and the reason why buyers and sellers walk through the door. And while they may be the ones that you signed the contracts with, they are not going to be the ones who are helping you to sell your home.

Instead, you are going to be working with their junior agents. These real estate agents may not have all of the experience and networking established that the top agent has and you may not be able to receive the quality of service that you are expecting when you signed with that agency.

During the negotiation process you have two people with very different goals. On the one hand you have the seller who is looking for someone to buy their home and they are hoping to make some money on the deal. On the other hand you have the buyer who is looking for the best home at the cheapest price. And then in the middle who do you have left? The Realtor who is just looking at trying to get this process completed as quickly as possible so they can earn their commission.

When a Realtor comes to a seller and says that he should lower the asking price in order to make the home more appealing, the seller doesn't realize that this is done to try and speed up the sale of the home so it will make the Realtor's job easier. So they may give into the Realtor's request and lower the price. The Realtor earns their commission, the buyer gets their home at a lower price and the seller is the one who loses equity and may be only barely able to cover the mortgage and all the costs that are involved with selling a home.

The only time when you may see a seller being able to receive their asking price without any issues from either the buyer or the Realtor is when there is a sellers' market. But there is rarely a time when there are more buyers than there are homes available. In fact, according to many Realtors, it is a seller's market when they are trying to convince the homeowner to list their home with them and then miraculously it is a buyer's market when a bid is received and negotiations are about to take place.

In addition, Realtor's commissions are only slightly affected when you drop your selling price. When you drop your home by $30,000 you have just lost $30,000 while your Realtor loses only $450. That is why they are so willing to convince you to continuously drop your price. If the Realtors had a personal stake involved and their commissions were tied more dramatically to the selling price, I imagine you would see Realtors trying to convince more homeowners to increase the price instead of decreasing it.

There are some sellers who are unrealistic when it comes to the selling price for their home. I have seen many homeowners who are asking way too much for a home that isn't worth even close to the assumed value. The value the sellers are using to create the price is not the appraised value of the home. They are looking at many different factors. Perhaps they invested a lot of money in the home and are hoping to be able to see some profit from that investment.

Or they are looking at the value of the home when they bought it and don't understand that the condition of the home has altered or the market has shifted enough that the value has since decreased.

There are some legitimate instances where a Realtor might be right when they say that a homeowner should lower the asking price. In most instances; however, it is simply a matter of laziness and greed. They're trying to get the most amount of money out of the least amount of work and they're doing it at your expense because it doesn't dramatically affect their commission.

When homeowners are unable to sell their home for a long period of time or have been frustrated by dealing with several different Realtors who are unable to produce results, they decide that they need to go another way. They decide it is probably time for them to sell their home on their own. What they may see as a solution may actually cause more problems.

Sell on Their Own

One benefit of a Realtor is that they understand what it takes to make improvements to a property so that it is more appealing to buyers. Many homeowners don't have this ability, may have poor taste when it comes to decor, and may not understand that if you want to sell your home, you should repaint those chipped walls, buy new carpeting for the stairs, and should probably have that leaky boiler fixed.

They just list their home in blissful ignorance and may not understand why no one is interested in buying their home. One person I know purchased their home as a cash deal. He thought he would fix up the place and then turn around and sell it for twice the amount that he bought it for. In the process of buying the home he didn't obtain a home inspection.

This was a serious problem because when he was looking to sell his home later a potential buyer did have a home inspection done. There were several code violations, issues with the foundation, issues with the heating system and other problems that would not only discourage buyers, but also discourage bankers from financing anyone who is interested in purchasing that property.

He ended up spending thousands of dollars more than he had planned in order to make the property up to code and viable to potential buyers. Not only was he not able to sell the home for twice what it was worth, he was barely able to make money on the deal by the time he was done because of all of the repairs he had to do.

Now I'm not saying that you have to have a home inspection done before you sell a house and I am not saying that every home has thousands of dollars of home repairs that need to be done before it will be appealing to buyers. What I am saying is that many people don't understand that most buyers aren't willing to purchase a property "as is." And if you are looking at getting anywhere near your asking price, you may have to invest some money into your home before people are willing to buy it.

Another potential problem that can occur when people try to sell their home on their own is that many homeowners don't know how to go about marketing their home and finding potential buyers.

There are many different ways an owner can advertise their home. There has been an increase in for sale by owner companies. In Canada ComFree and The Property Guys are just two of the well-known For Sale by Owner businesses that have cropped up over the years. All these guys are willing to help you sell your home at a much lower cost than using a Realtor. They can cost approximately $100-$1,500, depending on the package you choose.

A possible option that is now available for many homeowners that want to sell privately that was not available before is the MLS system. It used to be that only Realtors were able to access and list properties on this database. Because the Competition Board has eliminated some of the restrictions on the site, homeowners now have the option of paying a fee to discount brokerages or CommFree so that your home can be listed on that database. This allows you access to all the buyers who are doing their own research looking for potential homes and helps to expand your market reach.

For those who are looking for an even less expensive method to advertise your home you can go to Kijiji and Craigslist. You can create an ad for free and even include photos to help make your home look more appealing to potential buyers. Another free method of marketing your home is by leveraging social media. Communicating with followers and friends on the Internet can help spread the word that you are selling your home and might lead to finding a buyer who is looking for a new place in your area.

You are not the only person selling your home on these free sites. Realtors, for sale by owner companies and individuals leverage Kijiji and Craigslist to sell their home. This means that you have to be able to be good with words and create an ad that will stand out from all the other ads that are also selling homes. If you don't have marketing experience and if you are a poor speller you may not be able to attract the attention you need to sell your home with this method.

If you managed to develop an effective ad and create the right asking price for your home it should sell fairly quickly. If, however, you don't understand the market, have too much sentimental value attached to the home, or have no idea about the current appraised value of your property, you may run into the problem of having your home staying on the market for a long period of time.

A third issue that may occur when trying to sell a home on your own is that most people aren't good salesmen. When potential buyers come to take a look at the home, homeowners don't know how to play up the good points of the home to make it sound appealing. They also don't understand negotiations and may end up dropping the price too far in order to make a deal when they probably could have held firm and ended up with more money at the end of the day.

For those who sell the home quickly, congratulations; however, you are still only getting money now instead of using a method that will help you to get money every month for the next three years. If you are unable to sell your home through a Realtor and have no success selling the home on your own, you may find that your next option is to try to rent your home.

Rent Out a Home

People who rent out their home usually do so for one of two reasons. The first reason why you may want to rent out your home is because you weren't able to sell it and you need to have some kind of income instead of having the property stay vacant. People with more of an investor's mindset may turn their home into a rental as a way to make extra money.

These people may even purchase several different homes and turn them into rentals as a way to make a decent income and achieve a higher quality lifestyle.

An issue with renting your home is that, as with selling your home on your own, you have to market your property. This time you are looking for potential renters and not buyers, but you still have the same avenues such as Kijiji and Craigslist. In this case, you want to word your ad in a way that attracts the right type of tenants.

It is not always easy to find quality tenants. If the tenants don't pay the rent or if they damage the house while they are there, you have to make a decision on when and how to evict them.

There many other decisions that you need to make when deciding to rent your home. You need to decide whether or not you want to accept smokers and pet owners. Many landlords who accept smokers require extra rent and security deposit. This is because people who smoke may end up damaging the carpets with cigarette burns and the smoke of the cigarette stains the walls. This may force the homeowner to repaint the property after the tenant leaves so that you can rent the home to another person.

There are many different decisions that revolve around pet owners. Some landlords say that only cats and perhaps small dogs will be allowed on the premises. Other landlords allow all sized dogs, as well as cats and most landlords increase the amount of the security deposit if they do allow pets. This extra amount hopefully will be able to cover such expenses as carpets that are ruined from urine, doorframes that were chewed on and floors that were dug up by claws.

Another question is when you receive a call from an interested tenant how do you screen him or her to make sure that they are a quality choice? The best way to do that is to verify employment and do a background check. Verifying employment isn't difficult, it is a matter of making a phone call and most the time the employer is willing to give you the information you require.

You can also contact any previous landlords that the individual may have had before coming to you. One possible problem that you may run into is that their current landlord may not give you accurate information. Why would they not want to help you out? It is a matter of selfishness. They may be so sick of the current tenant that they will say anything they have to in order to get rid of them.

So you should always contact the landlord previous to their current landlord. They are the most often willing to provide accurate information that will give you a good idea of what this tenant is like.

You can also ask for references, both personal and professional. This would be like something you would see on a job application. But just as with a job application, these potential tenants will be contacting the references ahead of time to obtain permission to use their name. While on that call there is nothing to say that they won't persuade the reference to provide positive information in order for them to get into the home. Many employers find that they hire candidates with impeccable references only to find out that the person is lazy, unengaged and rarely shows up to work. As a landlord you may have no better luck using references than employers do.

Checking their credit and doing a background check is a beneficial way to obtain an accurate picture about a potential tenant. Each of these applications cost money however and you may not be able to afford to screen 20 tenants with this process in order to find one possible candidate.

When you are renting a home you are responsible for all maintenance and repairs. Some homeowners will make an agreement with their tenant to deduct some of the money from the rent if the individual is willing to shovel, mow and do basic yard work. You have to have a tenant who is willing to do this work and do it right. Even if they do the work you still have to supply the tools and materials for them to do the landscaping for you.

You have to do all of the rest of the maintenance and repairs yourself or hire someone to do them for you. And when you're renting a home to tenants your time is not your own. You can get calls at three in the morning because your tenant stopped up the toilet and they don't know how to use a plunger. Sometimes things just break and they never seem to break during the day when you have nothing else to do. Instead, they like to break when it's the middle of the night, the weather is absolutely atrocious, or you have plans to leave on vacation.

One solution that many people will turn to if they are renting their home and are tired of being a landlord is a property management company. Hiring a property management company to look after a rental is not always the best answer. They can be costly, especially if you don't have a good one.

A good property manager is worth their weight in gold, provided they are saving you money each month by reducing all the other expenses that go along with renting out your home. For most, it isn't necessarily the 10% the property managers charge each month that is the problem, it is the additional repairs, maintenance, fees for showing and filling the property, vacancies, etc. Finding a good property manager can be tough. It can take some trial and error to find a good one. I have also never heard of a property manager guaranteeing the rents.

Although I don't manage other people's properties in the traditional sense, I am friends with the owners of a property management company and have a full understanding of how they make money.

One possible problem with property management companies is that they can do a terrible job at screening tenants. They also nickel and dime you to death on the fees. I have a friend who used to work for a property management company and she has told me on several occasions about the decisions someone made to put people in the home that was from a group who is known to trash properties, yet they did it anyway.

The reason for this is because most property management companies are more interested in keeping the properties filled than they are at truly screening the tenants. Always having tenants in the property is the way that these companies keep their contracts. No landlord wants to pay the company for maintaining a vacant rental. So while they may guarantee that they do a thorough screening process when reviewing applicants this may not always be the case.

And whether you are using a property management company or maintaining the property on your own a vacant rental costs money. Not only do you have to advertise the property in order to find new tenants, but you also have to pay for the utilities while the location is vacant. This is on top of any repairs or improvements that you need to do to the property in order to fix the damage done by previous tenants.

In order to be a good landlord and be able to do your job effectively you need to be good at documentation and paperwork. This is more than being able to draft a legally binding lease agreement. This is also about giving a receipt when the tenant pays the rent, documenting any potential issues that you may have had with your tenant, and keeping receipts of all the repairs and work that you may have done on the property.

All of this different documentation and paperwork can be time-consuming. Some landlords turn to property management companies who have the experience and documentation necessary to create leases that are legally binding. They also have the processes in place to make sure that all work is done properly and that everything is documented the way that it should be.

In terms of the law it is not always about what we would consider right and wrong. It is about having the right contracts and having all the information listed correctly. While there are templates available for lease and monthly rental agreements, you can even download them online, they don't always cover every contingency. If you alter the contract template in order to compensate for your particular needs, your changes may not be legally binding. In order to make sure that you are protecting the tenants' rights you need to be able to understand the provincial residential tenancy act. You also need to be able to understand any potential legal changes for your specific province.

A possible solution is to hire a lawyer on retainer. This way if a problem does come up you will have representation and they may be able to help you draft the documents you need in order to rent out your home. Keeping a lawyer on retainer is expensive and just because they have experience with real estate this doesn't necessarily mean that they have experience with rentals. You need to make sure that if you do have a lawyer on retainer he has the right type of experience and will be able to help you if you get into a situation where you need to of the act or start legal action against one of your tenants.

So, we have covered the three main avenues that most people consider when they are looking to sell their home. First they try with the Realtor or sell their home on their own. This isn't always easy and can have many drawbacks. Most homeowners lose money when they try to sell their home and are lucky if they break even. Even if they do manage to make decent money on the sale they are making the money once and do not have the opportunity of receiving money every year for the next three years.

If they are not successful selling their home through a Realtor or on their own, a homeowner may decide to rent their home. Renting a home can be a very time-consuming and expensive process. If you don't do it right you can end up with a poor quality tenant who at best may not pay their rent and at worst damage the home, causing you to invest a significant amount of money on repairs.

You may face long stretches of time when the home is vacant, but you still have to cover the cost of utilities. Property management companies advertise that they can help reduce the stress of being a landlord. This is not always the case because there are property management companies that are not good at their jobs and if they are a good company they are too expensive for many homeowners to be able to afford.

These are the three options that most people believe are the only choices available to them when they are looking to sell or move out of their home. They don't understand that there is an alternative solution that will actually help them save money and even make money in the process. That option is to rent to own your home for three years and then sell it.

Alternative Solution – Rent to Own

As I mentioned in the last chapter the majority of homeowners I met with after contracting me on my "Gold Mine" ad did not even realize there were services out there and available to them to turn their homes into a rent to own. However, for the past four years I have only ever been offering one option to the homeowner, but later on in this book I am going to discuss three different options available to you, the homeowner.

As I pull back the curtain on the whole RTO industry and shed light on the shady investors by educating you how the process works and how ethical investors and homeowners operate, you are going to know exactly how much money is to be made on rent to owns. By doing this you will also see how my company makes its money and how much we make. For most people, opening up how and how much we make on rent to owns is considered taboo when talking to homeowners or tenant buyers. I will never apologize for making money and putting food on the table because just like you, I'm trying to make an honest living.

Rent to Own Revolution

The *Rent to Own Revolution* has begun and it's going to make some people a great deal of money.

As we touched on in Chapter 1 there has been a dramatic increase in the demand for the number of people looking to get into a rent to own and the demand is steadily increasing, as a result of the banks making it harder to qualify for a mortgage, homeowners wanting to keep more of their equity from the sale of their home and the increase in investors being trained and promoting rent to owns, creating the "Perfect Storm,".

What Does This Mean To You?

You may not even realize it but you have the unique ability to make bucket loads of money. Ok....maybe not bucket loads, but up to $60,000+ more than your traditional sale today, from what was probably the biggest investment you have ever made in your life; your home!

And that is what this book is all about.

I want to show you how you can leverage your home during this "Perfect Storm" of social and economic forces to:

- Maximize the money you make from your home
- Access your equity now while your home makes you money
- Get people who are willing to fix your home at their own expense
- Get someone else to pay down your mortgage for you
- Sell your home for top dollar and help another family in the process

The ability for individuals to qualify for a traditional mortgage has become increasingly difficult. As a result of the financial crisis of 2008-2009 the banks have tightened up their lending practices when it comes to homes. Now, people like you and me (who never would have had a chance before) get to play the role of the banks and Realtors, taking advantage in the best way possible.

They are using their home as an investment vehicle to help someone else get into home ownership while they let their money work for them. They are also taking advantage of someone else paying down their mortgage, covering the costs of repairs and maintenance and selling at top dollar without having to pay a Realtor.

Let's face it, the money you are going to make instead of the bank isn't going to break them, but it will definitely go a long way to helping you make a better life for your family and loved ones, especially if you were to repeat this process every 3-5 years. Just think of the retirement fund you would have!

This system has already started helping create its fair share of success-stories. Folks like Chaang Y. and Liz N. just to name a few.

Chaang Y is an ironworker who purchased a three bedroom townhouse and decided to have two roommates. Just after one short year he had had enough of living with other people, yet the home was too big just for him. With four years remaining on the term of his mortgage, no increase in the property value and the dated interior Chaang Y. was looking at taking a loss if he were to sell today.

By putting his home into this system, Chaang Y. was able to get entire main floor of the home renovated at no cost to him, and get great tenants for the next three years who are going to pay for all repairs and maintenance under $1,000 per instance and he will sell it for more than he paid in three years without the expense of a Realtor, saving him $10,000. Chaang Y. also gets to benefit from three years of mortgage pay down that will see him put an extra $18,000+ in his pocket.

Liz N. on the other hand is a real estate investor with a couple of rental properties. She wanted to get into some more real estate but did not want to deal with any more issues that come with your typical tenants.

Liz decided to buy a home and put it into this system and started taking big checks to the bank from day one. She received a $15,000 non-refundable payment from the tenants before they moved in and is making $750 per month in cash flow each and every month. Her tenants are responsible for all repairs under $1,500 per instance, so unless something major happens to the property Liz will never spend another cent on the property. In two years when her tenants buy her home Liz will walk away with over $40,000 profit just from the appreciation and mortgage pay down. The total profit over the two-year period will be $73,000.

The best part about stories like those of Chaang Y. and Liz N. is that their levels of success are nowhere near mandatory for profitability. In the traditional method of selling properties they would have given 7% of the first $100,000 and 3% of the rest to the Realtor. In the traditional rental game, Liz would be worried about the home going vacant, being on call for the dreaded calls because they didn't know how to change a light bulb or unclog a toilet. Nowadays, using this system they worry less and make more.

This is Quite a Game Changer

On one end we have investors looking for an easier way to make money in real estate without all the struggles, risks and headaches associated with the profession; on the other hand we have home owners who don't want to or can't invest money into their home for renovations, or just want to make more money from the sale of their home. They both win at the expense of the banks and Realtors. Plus, they are helping some great people be able to get into home ownership that may not have otherwise had the opportunity to buy a home. The tenant buyers love this. They are happy.

Homeowners can get someone into their home quickly, instead of having it sit on the market for months only to pay someone when it sells. One thing we haven't touched on yet, but we will further along in the book is how the homeowner can get the majority of their equity out of the home upfront and still make money on the home. In other words, they make more money, can get their equity immediately and have to deal with fewer issues than your typical landlord. The homeowners love this. They are happy.

This is today's new real estate landscape. It is not the speculating of 2005/6 and selling in 2007, but there will be some serious money made in addition to what already has been.

But before we cover how you can tap into your share of the *Rent to own Revolution* let's first go through the five reasons you want to use this system of renting for three years before selling.

Section 2 - 5 Reasons to Rent to Own

Chapter 4

ACCESS TO EQUITY

"I think the key indicator for wealth is not good grades, work ethic, or IQ. I believe it's relationships. Ask yourself two questions: How many people do I know, and how much ransom money could I get for each one?"

- Jarod Kintz

In the first section we covered a great deal of information. First, I explained about the *Rent to Own Revolution* and how it has been created because of the Perfect Storm. First is your and other homeowners' relationship with Realtors. Because so many people are losing so much of their equity to banks, they are trying to keep what little they have left. It is bad enough that buyers tend to take a piece of that equity because they negotiate for a lower selling price, and you aren't always in a position to tell them no.

You are looking for a way to sell your home, but the situation with the housing market has made it difficult. The banks make it difficult to access the equity in your home, home values have shifted, and many people are still dealing with upside down mortgages. You may feel that there is no way to sell your home and get the cash you need to put a down payment on a new home.

Another aspect of the Perfect Storm is that people who are looking to obtain a mortgage have difficulty qualifying. This is because banks have already tightened the restrictions regarding how you can qualify to obtain a loan. Plus, there is talk that they will tighten these restrictions even further in the near future due to the fact that house values continue to rise, but people's disposable income hasn't managed to keep pace with these costs.

The last part of the storm is increased training of investors. While there are good trainers and bad ones, good students and unethical people, the main result of all this training is that more people are interested in rent to own. This has increased the exposure of this option and gives me the perfect opportunity to show you how you can sell your home and make the money you deserve.

In Chapter 3 we covered the options that people believe they are limited to when they want to sell their home. We talked about the most popular option, which is selling through a Realtor. We discussed how a Realtor not only takes a large portion of your hard earned equity, but how also they don't always do everything they should to help make sure you sell your home quickly and at a fair price. Realtors so often want you to lower the price of your home, not so that they can get a good deal, but so that the Realtor can speed up the sale.

Also in Chapter 3 we took a look at an option that has become popular since people have become sick of Realtors and are trying to save money. More people are trying to sell their home on their own and more for sale by owner companies have popped into existence in response to this trend. The problem with selling a home by yourself is that you so often don't have the market reach, salesmanship or negotiation skills to sell the home at a decent price. And, if you haven't set the right price for the home, it can sit on the market for months.

With the current economic situation and so few qualified buyers, many people turn to the third option that we covered in Chapter 3, renting the home. While this can help you receive an income from what would be an empty property, there are many issues with becoming a landlord. Poor quality tenants, maintenance and legal problems can occur when renting the property and you also will have to deal with periods when the house stands empty between tenants and you have to pay utilities without receiving income from the home.

People have used these three options because they thought they didn't have any other choice. They didn't understand that there was a fourth option that can help you find a buyer, earn more money, and not have to worry about repairs or maintenance fees that are standard with renting or selling a home. This option is renting your home for three years and then selling it to a newly qualified buyer.

In this section we are going to go into more detail about how homeowners benefit when they use the RTO option to sell their home. The five reasons to rent to own your home for three years and then sell it include:

- Access to Equity
- Selling Your Home for Top Dollar

- Someone Else Pays the Mortgage
- Someone Else Covers Repairs
- Money Doesn't Lie

In this chapter we are going to look at your equity and ways you can access it now. Traditionally, if you wanted immediate access to your equity you would sell your home, either on your own or through a Realtor. But there is a better way to get access to your equity now and make more money in the future while you wait three years to sell your home. And by using the rent to own method, you will also be receiving money in between.

It's almost as if I said: Which is more appealing to you: $75,000 now and nothing ever again or $75,000 now, more money every month and at least another $30,000 in three years, which would you pick?

For those of you who picked the second option, I agree with you. This is what I have been helping people do for the last four years. And, depending on your financial needs, I can also show you ways that you can access more of your equity up front.

REASON 1: Get Your Money Out of the House Now While it Makes You More Money in the Next Three Years

Probably one of the biggest reasons people sell their homes is the need for the equity from the property to buy another home or to use the money for some other reasons. The lending rules have changed considerably, making it tougher for homeowners to access the money in their home that is theirs.

Usually when you need to upsize, downsize or relocate their automatic thought is to sell your home, take the equity and go buy another home. But what if there was a way you could get equity out of your home and then make money on your home? Would that interest you? Even better, if you didn't have to worry about repairs, maintenance or vacancies as much as you would with a typical rental, would that peak your interest?

Ironically, the biggest reason people sell their homes is also one of the five reasons to turn your home into a rent to own and cash in on the impending revolution that is coming. What I'm going to teach you later on in this chapter you will never get from your bankers or your financial advisers, because they either don't know about it, don't understand it or just don't want you to do it because they can't make any money from you when you do this. I will touch on this a little bit later in the chapter.

Standard Method

With the current lending rules the way they are today you can only access up to 80% of the equity in your home. So if you have more than 20% equity, let's say for this example you have 30% equity, then you can go to your traditional bank, refinance the property and get 10% of your equity out of the property. Remember, the banks want you to have a minimum 20% equity in the property so they feel secure in their position holding the mortgage on your home.

To make things easier I'm going to walk through the financials of a particular home and a couple different scenarios so you can see things for yourself.

Current Home Value: $300,000

Mortgage Value: $210,000

Mortgage as a percentage of Value: 70%

Equity in Home: $90,000

Equity as a percentage of Value: 30%

Now for our example we need to sell the home. In this example we are going to have you use a traditional Realtor who is amazing at his/her job and gets you almost full price for your home. Here is how things would go with the sale of the home.

Selling Price: $298,000

Commission (7% on first $100k and 3% on the rest) $12,940

Net Selling Price: $285,060

Equity from the Sale: $75,060

Equity as a percentage of Value: 25%

So you can see you ended up losing 5% of your equity when you sold the home. You lost some to negotiations and the rest to the Realtor for their commissions. Just imagine if you only had 5% equity in your home; where would that leave you now? Well, like so many people these days who bought their home during the peak of the market in 2006/7 in Edmonton, they are faced with this exact scenario.

For many people, getting that $75,000 of equity so they can move on to buy their next home is worth the $15,000 they are giving away. Well if it wasn't why would so many people keep selling their homes with a traditional Realtor? The problem is they don't know of a better system or alternative that can get them the money they need in order to buy their next home while keeping more of the equity.

What I'm about to show you here will never be taught to you by your bank or your financial advisor, because they make less money from you, don't know of it or don't understand what I am about to show you next. I'm going to show you how you can get your $75,000 just as if you sold your home, but you get to keep your home and actually make more money with it over the next three years. There are going to be a few moving parts in this process, but it is much easier than you think.

Revolution Method

First thing you need to do is to refinance your home up to the maximum of 80% loan to value. You can do that through your traditional bank or talk to a mortgage broker to get the best rates possible. Let's take a look at how that looks after we get the home refinanced up to 80%.

Current Value: $300,000

Mortgage Value: $240,000

Mortgage as % of Value: 80%

Equity: $60,000

Equity as % of Value: 20%

Cash in Hand: $30,000

You financed it at a rate of 3.5% over 25 years.

So after you refinanced the home you ended up with $30,000 in the bank. Now for our example we are going to assume that isn't enough for the down payment you need on your next home, so you need to come up with some more. So instead of selling the home you decide you are going to take advantage of the revolution that is going on and turn your home into a rent to own.

In doing this you decide you want to help a family who has a good job, available cash and just some credit issues. After you put them through the process, which we will look at later in the book, they are ready to get into the home on a three year rent to own.

One of the benefits of RTO is you get to sell your home for a future price, which is generally higher than today's value for the home. To keep this example simple, let's say you are going to set the home price to be $315,000 at the end of three years. That means you expect the appreciation of the home to be 5% total over three years. This would be extremely low but it makes for easy calculations for my example.

Increasing the Down Payment

You can get some money up front from the person who is going to rent your home for three years and then buy. In most cases you can get 2%-3% of the purchase price; sometimes you can even get 5% of the purchase price. This would be their down payment for the future purchase of the home, which in our program is technically called a non-refundable option consideration.

If you need more equity upfront and you have decided to turn your home into a rent to own you can choose to only work with someone who already had the 5% down payment the banks required. Once you go through the qualification process, you sign the documents and they hand you the bank draft for $15,000. Let's take a look at your situation after that transpires.

Before Rent to Own:

Current Value: Unchanged at $300,000

Mortgage Value: Unchanged at $240,000

Mortgage as % of Value: 80%

Equity: 60,000

Equity as % of Value: 20%

CASH IN HAND: $30,000

After Rent to Own is signed:

Future Selling Price: $315,000

Option for Future Purchase (Down Payment):
$15,000

Balance Due Upon Sale in 3 years: $300,000

Current Mortgage Value: $240,000

Current Mortgage as % of Balance Due Upon Sale:
80%

Equity: $60,000

Equity as % of Balance Due Upon Sale: 20%

CASH IN HAND: $45,000

Now let's take a look at the numbers above. You can see the $15,000 they gave you upfront both came off the future selling price and also got put in your cash in hand account at the same time. As a result of increasing the future selling price of the home a reasonable amount, which also happened to be the amount of the down payment, the buyer still needs to pay you $300,000 at the close of the sale three years from now. You did not lose out on any equity, if anything you kept your equity and increased the cash in hand position so you can purchase your next home.

If you are thinking about the timing of all of this then I can tell you we generally sign up people for the rent to own homes about a month away from the time they actually get to move in. So with that, you get the money early and have time to move out of the home and into your new place.

At this point in time your cash in hand position is $30,000 less than if you just sold your home with a Realtor ($75,000-$45,000), however your overall position at this point in time has been increased by $30,000 ($60,000 (equity)+$45,000 (cash in hand)-$75,000(what you would get if you sold today)).

As it stands right now you are going to make $30,000 more than if you just sold your home, however, we haven't even considered cash flow and mortgage pay downs, which we will get into in later chapters. Right now, it is all about getting your equity out of your home while you can still make money with your property over the next three years.

So as it stands we are still $30,000 short to get you $75,000 cash in hand, which is what you would get by selling your home through a Realtor. Now this is the part I mentioned to you earlier in the chapter that you will never have a banker or financial adviser tell you about. I only recommend this strategy if you absolutely need the $30,000, otherwise don't bother as it will eat into your profits on the rent to own. It really boils down to what you are going to use the money for.

I'm not going to preach about money management; however I will tell you that all money comes at a cost. Whether it is your money that you spend, which means it cost you the opportunity to use it to make money, or it is money that you borrow, which obviously costs you the interest.

I will explain to you how you are going to get the extra $30,000 out but I'm going to tell you the same thing I tell all my investors and coaching students. Only do this if you absolutely need the money and you are going to use it to invest in something that is going to make you more interest than it costs.

Using Other People's RRSP's As Mortgages

The government encourages us to save for retirement, especially by investing or saving in, among other things, Registered Retirement Savings Plan, or "RRSP."

Wall Street investment firms will always encourage you to invest through an RRSP. And they're right – RRSPs can be one of the best vehicles for investment, especially given their tax-favored nature. Unfortunately, few of these firms will tell you about the "Self-Directed RRSP."

What they should call the RRSP they tout is "The RRSP where we dictate what you can put in it." The government will not allow you to put some investments into your RRSP. There are lots of investments that the government will allow, but the fee-hungry investment firms don't want you to know about these, since they don't get their fat fees from them!

You can invest in real estate through an RRSP, but probably not through the one you already have. You must have a "self-directed" RRSP in order to invest in real estate using your RRSP. With this RRSP, you can defer your tax payments, or even pay no taxes at all in your investments.

Why would you or a potential investor want to invest in real estate versus the stock market, which is a traditional form of investing many people use to fund their retirement? Well, you may want to ask that to many people in both Canada and the United States who are now facing going into retirement with nothing because their RRSP's and 401Ks, which are the same as our RRSP, was heavily invested in stocks when the market took a nose dive in the 2000s.

Return on Investment

Jan 1, 2000 – June 30, 2010

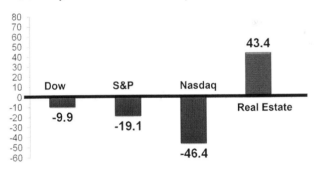

Advantages of Real Estate Investing

- Tangibility
- Investment leverage
- Control over management
- Inflation hedge
- Strong returns
- Low risk
- Preferential task treatment

Inflation is the buying power of your money. Real estate investing is a hedge against inflation because home prices, absent a bubble, mirror the consumer price index faithfully.

Real estate investing also offers you leverage. If you have $100,000 and you are looking for an investment that will give you the most leverage what is your best option?

- Stocks, mutual funds and RRSPs will give you $100,000
- Gold or silver will give you $100,000
- Real Estate, however, give you the ability to buy $500,000 or more

You can invest in the following types of real estate through a "self-directed" RRSP:

- Single-family homes
- Apartments
- Mobile Homes
- Commercial Property
- Raw land
- Real estate notes

- Mortgages
- Tax liens

This is an option some people have used to buy their own home. While it is recommended that you have at least $100,000 or more in the account, you can use this as an option to getting a traditional mortgage with the bank. With the RRSP mortgage in this case, you are paying yourself back the money every month.

In order to use this method, however, you not only need to have built $100,000 in your retirement account, which takes most people time to build, you also have to be able to hold your retirement off for the 25-30 years it takes for you to pay yourself back. That is why the option of finding an arm's length investor is a faster and more viable option for most homeowners who need to buy a new home and don't have enough equity to make a down payment.

There are two types of mortgages that can be held within retirement accounts such as RRSPs and RRIFs arm's length and non-arm's length.

The term "arm's length" is used by CRA and refers to how closely or distant the borrower / property owner and the lender are in relation to each other.

For example, for a borrower, the following people are considered

- **Non-arm's length** – brother, sister, parents, spouse (either common law or by marriage), your own children (including adopted)

- **Arm's length** – friends, strangers, uncles, aunts, cousins

This means that for a mortgage to be classified by CRA as arm's length, an individual could borrow mortgage funds from the RRSPs of their friends, strangers, uncles, aunts, and cousins, but not a brother, sister, parent, spouse or child.

You may be asking at this point why an arm's length RRSP mortgage is preferable to one that is non-arm's length. It is not that it isn't possible for the borrower to be an immediate family member and still receive a RRSP mortgage. It is because these types of mortgages are heavily administered and restricted. The arm's length RRSP gives you and the investor the freedom to negotiate the terms of the agreement.

Difference Between the Two Types of RSP Mortgages

- Non –Arm's Length
  - Lending to yourself or direct family
  - Expensive
  - Must be CMHC insured
  - Must be paid back
  - Must Qualify
- Arm's Length
  - Lending to non-direct family members
  - Terms are variable
  - Payment is variable
  - No Qualification

For a detailed description of CRA's definition of 'arm's length', please refer to interpretation bulletin # IT-419R2 at http://www.cra-arc.gc.ca/E/pub/tp/it419r2/

All investments within retirement accounts, including arm's length mortgages, must be managed by financial institutions. For RRSP Mortgages, the financial institution acts as a trustee for the account holder and manages the mortgage on the private lender's behalf. There are only three or four in Canada.

- Canadian Western Trust
- Olympia Trust
- B2B Trust

Trustee Structure

Real Estate Investor Or Home Owner

Negotiate Terms

Private Lenders – Anyone with RSP's

SDRSP

Via Lawyers

OLYMPIA
TRUST COMPANY

Trustee

ioffersolutions
Real Estate Services Inc.

For example:

- Tim has a self-directed RRSP account with Olympia Trust
- Tony wants to borrow his RRSP money in the form of a mortgage
- Tim's financial institution acts as his trustee for the transaction

Private RRSP Mortgage lenders are an excellent way to finance a property with little to no hassle, and with terms and conditions favorable to the borrower. Anyone who doesn't want to deal with banks, has lost their job, or needs down payment money should consider using them to finance property.

The following list is a brief overview of some ways RRSP Mortgages can be used to finance property:

- **Buying property** – reduce or eliminate the need for bank financing, as a substitute for a down payment, mortgage insurance, or a joint venture partner
- **Refinancing** – pay for renovations, buy more property, buy out any partners
- **Selling property** – make your property easy for people to buy with no qualifying mortgages

Advantages of RSP Mortgages

- You negotiate with the lender
  - Payments can be monthly, quarterly or yearly
  - Pay interest only option

- o Balloon payment option
- o Stepped payment option
- Variable rates
- No qualifying
- No credit check
- Open mortgage
- No appraisal or other red tape
- No broker fees
- No down payment verification
- Low set-up fees (Only pay trustee and lawyer)

A lawyer will handle the transaction just like he would any other real estate transaction. He or she will register the mortgage on the title and take care of the title and property insurance.

As with any mortgage financing, great care must be taken to ensure you can afford to make the payments as well as, at the end of the term, repay the original amount borrowed.

In addition, you should also know:

- exactly how mortgages work
- how to structure RRSP Mortgages to their advantage
- what to do when the mortgage term has ended, and exactly how to fill out the trustee paperwork

What steps are involved in getting it going?

After reviewing a potential RRSP investment lender's current situation, via the interview information gathering process, and after they have reviewed your proposal with their team of advisors and are ready to go, the next seven simple steps are all that is required.

The steps are:

1. Open a Self-Directed RRSP account that MUST be able to deal in "Arms-length" mortgages
2. Put contribution in place or transfer funds
3. Prepare instructions to place mortgage, including (independent legal advice letter)
4. Wait for the funds to be forwarded to the lawyer
5. Register the mortgage on the property
6. Watch your RRSP account grow
7. Repeat the process.

Producing consistent, predictable RRSP returns through this Self Directed RRSP strategy allows investors the opportunity to take advantage of superior tax sheltered R.O.I. results, and cash in on Canadian real estate. They get a great return on a great property and you get the property! It is a win-win scenario for both of you.

To get the remaining $30,000 cash out of the home we are going to have you find someone you know, but not directly related to (for regulatory purposes) and ask them if they would like to turn $30,000 worth of their RRSPs into a mortgage, for which in the example, you are going to pay them 10% simple interest on the original amount. For more detailed instructions on using RRSPs as mortgages please be sure to email your book receipt to receipts@RentToOwnRevolution.com to get access to the members' area to access all the resources that go along with this book.

Now, let's take a look at the current situation after you found a friend who was eager to make 10% interest on their RRSPs after they lost 20-40% of their total value in the markets since 2006. Here is how you are sitting now:

After RRSP Mortgage is registered:

Future Selling Price: $315,000

Option for Future Purchase: $15,000

Balance Due Upon Sale: $300,000

1st Mortgage Value: $240,000

RRSP Mortgage Value: $30,000

Mortgages as % of Balance Due Upon Sale: 90%

Equity: $30,000

Equity as % of Balance Due Upon Sale: 10%

CASH IN HAND: $75,000

There are a few things you need to keep in mind as a precaution when using RRSPs as mortgages. First, always try to negotiate with the owner of the RRSP to allow you to pay all the principle and interest into the RRSP account as a balloon payment at the end. This way you don't have to worry about monthly payments or cutting into your monthly cash flow, should there be any. Obviously this takes the pressure off you when it comes repaying the mortgage.

Second thing to keep in mind is that you should only do this with a clear exit strategy of selling the home. Remember, the mortgage will come due so you want to make sure the funds are there to pay back into your friend's RRSP account. Using this strategy on long term buy rent and hold properties is not advisable unless you can finance the entire house with the RRSP mortgage, in which case you would be making monthly payments back to the RRSP account.

Lastly, always have an RRSP mortgage term longer than the term of the rent to own. That way, should the RTO not go through as expected you still have some time to extend the RTO term, sell the home or do another rent to own. The RRSP Mortgages are usually open, so you can pay them back at any time.

I have taught this strategy to many investors who have embraced the strategy to free up their equity so they can buy more properties and reinvest. Again, they only do this on properties they have turned into rent to owns and they aren't part of their long-term buy rent and hold strategy.

Reasons Why Investors Like To Use This Strategy

- Real Estate has a better track record over stocks, traditional RRSPs and mutual funds
- Real Estate investing is a hedge against inflation
- The secret to real estate investing is leverage
- Think like an investor

- o Everything cash flows
- o Most important thing is ROI
- o If ROI is good enough money will be there
- Buy for cash flow
- Have a strategy to get money out of the deal fast
- Use earned income strategies to invest in long term buy rent and holds

One such investor, Don, had purchased a couple of properties for me for the sole purpose of my company turning them into rent to owns. Now Don has a great job and is looking at having his money work for him with hopes he can passively build up a second stream of income through his real estate investing holdings. Now Don is diverse and has properties in US and in Canada, some buy rent and holds and others are structured, as rent to owns.

The investments Don has with my company are RTO projects. They were put into our guaranteed program, meaning my company rented them from Don with the option to purchase, then turned around and did the rent to own on the properties. This way Don was guaranteed to get his rent each and every month without delay, as it was my company paying the rent.

We also looked after all the management and the maintenance and repairs up to a certain value. With this model the home owner or investor only deals with my company and never has anything to do with the tenant buyers. It is our job to make everything work.

Just like with any investor, when you keep putting 20-25% down to buy properties you eventually run out of money. That is just what happened in Don's situation. He had done well getting into investments that were set to make him great cash flow, good return on investment and best of all Don never had to manage any of the projects. Now, however, Don was out of cash and couldn't invest in any other opportunities.

Now since Don was in my investor circle he would come to as many of the events I would host in Edmonton as possible. I would generally get between 40-80 people out to an education session when I wanted to teach others on some of the strategies we were doing or had knowledge in.

On one of these nights I did a session on using other people's RRSPs as mortgages to free up your equity so you could use it to buy more real estate. After the event Don was interested in doing just that, freeing up some of his equity in the RTO projects and doing some more investing.

Since I had a fairly diverse network in the Edmonton area I knew of many real estate investors who had RRSPs of their own who couldn't use them on their own properties and were looking for other people's projects to invest in. One such couple, Nina and Dave was actively looking to get their RRSPs out of the mutual fund market and into some solid investments that was backed by an actual asset, not just paper.

As an investor herself, Nina was aware of the process to turn her RRSPs into mortgages and had started the process to have her RRSPs transferred to one of the four companies that actually does this, so when she found the right investment she would be ready to go.

The process was simple; she called a company like Olympia Trust and asked to set up a self-directed RRSP account then gave that company the details of where her funds were currently held, along with the account information. That was it; she would be notified when the RRSP's were transferred. They never had to be cashed in, she wasn't taxed on the process, and all she did was change the company who was going to act as her Trustee for the RRSPs.

Once Don and Nina connected they went through the two rent to owns Don had with me and Nina agreed to place a certain amount of RRSPs on one of the projects at an agreed upon interest rate so Don could free up some of his equity and invest in some other projects. All the negotiations were between Don and Nina, no one else ever needed to be involved.

As the owner of the RRSPs Nina is like the bank, she gets to pick and choose who she "qualifies" to lend her money to. She evaluated the opportunities, where the properties were, the price points, the deals themselves then made her decision if she was going to use her RRSPs on one of the projects and if so, which one.

Once they agreed and came to terms they got together and filled out a short application form laying out the agreement that went to the lawyer and the Trustee Company, like an Olympia Trust where Nina's RRSPs where held. After a few weeks everything was done. Nina's RRSPs were now turned into a mortgage that was registered on the title of Don's rent to own investment house and Don received a check from the lawyer in the amount of the RRSP Mortgage.

For Nina, all it cost her was a few hundred dollars to set everything up with the Trustee Company and for Don it was the cost of having the mortgage documents prepared and registered by the lawyer. For both parties the process was very simple. Be sure to check in the member's area for more details on how you can do this with your RRSPs.

Money Against Equity

You can also find someone to lend the money against the equity. This can be pricy but I have lent money for equity (about 90% of the equity) in exchange for renting the home for three years and then buying it for what is left owing on the mortgages. If you can structure something like that it can usually happen quite quickly.

Not Enough Equity to Sell the Home Right Now

There are times when you need to sell you home but you don't have any equity built up. If you bought a home three years ago and your company transfers you to a new location, you may need to sell your current home but you haven't had time to build much equity. Not only will you have to find an alternate method to come up with a down payment for your new home, you could face other problems as well.

For instance, if you were using the old method of selling your home, you would have to pay Realtors commissions and payout penalties. You may even need to find money to make repairs on the home to make it more appealing to buyers.

That's too much money for most people to have to come up with on short notice. The solution: instead of taking a loss, paying Realtors, payout penalties and even repairs, the best bet is to turn it into a rent to own for 2-3 years then sell, giving you time to have the mortgage paid down.

You will even be able to receive some cash for a down payment with the money the tenant buyer gives you for their down payment. As with the situation where you need more access to your equity, if you decide to only deal with potential tenant buyers who have 5% of the purchase price, you will have the ability to use that money for your own move.

So there are many different ways that turning your home into a rent to own will give you more access to your money. If you need equity out of your house now to move on to the next phase of your life you can get some money up front from the person going to rent your home and buy it in the future by asking them for a down payment towards the future purchase price. You can receive anywhere from 2% to 5% of the purchase price as a down payment.

Another way that you can receive more of the equity in your home now by using the rent to own strategy is to use other people's RRSPs registered against the equity in your home to get the cash. You are obligated to pay back into the RRSP with interest, and you would do so when the home sells, but it is a way to get your cash now. This is how I structure many of my deals with my investors.

After they buy the home for me in order to help a family buy into a rent to own, we find some RRSPs to register against the home so the investor can pull the majority of their down payment back, putting them in a position to buy another property and having lowered their risk on the investment. You can do the same thing with your property.

You may want to look at finding someone who you will lend you money against the equity. This is an expensive choice, but if you need the money and can find someone to do this for you, it is an option.

And renting the home for three years and selling it is also beneficial if you have a situation where you have to sell your home before you have built enough equity. You have the breathing room to pay down the mortgage, increase the equity and avoid the penalties of an early payout.

While we have discussed this benefit of RTOs, it is important to understand that accessing the money now shouldn't be the determining factor to sell the home. There are many other benefits of using this method and we will continue that discussion in the future chapters in this book.

The aspect of looking for someone who is willing to offer you a RRSP mortgage to have more cash on hand or money in exchange for equity comes at a cost. These strategies will reduce your overall profit that you will receive by renting the home for three years and then selling it. You should only use them if you have an exit strategy and an urgent need for the money sooner rather than later.

How much money will you be able to earn by taking advantage of the *Rent to Own Revolution*? You will be able to see the benefits laid out for you in the next chapter. In Chapter 5 I am going to show you how you can sell your home for top dollar using this method. I am going to take you through it step by step and show you a comparison of what happens when you sell your home using the traditional method versus the rent to own strategy.

Renting your home for three years and then selling it will help you receive consistent income and a better selling price than you will using the traditional method to sell your home. The option of obtaining your equity now should only be an added benefit, not the main reason to sell your home using the traditional method or rent to own method.

Chapter 5

SELL YOUR HOME FOR TOP DOLLAR

"By trying we can easily endure adversity. Another man's, I mean."--Mark Twain

Let's face it, you work hard for your money and it sucks when you sell your home and you end up paying $10,000-$20,000 of your equity to a Realtor. I know how you feel, because before I got into real estate investing I bought and sold my very first house and I ended up spending a couple thousand dollars getting it show ready, at least better than it was, and walked away after the sale with no money.

My Story as a Comparison to the Revolution Method

Back in 2000, I was living in Edmonton with my friend Shelly. We'd gone in together on a rental along with my brother, though he was often away working at Fort McMurray. It was a great house: It had plenty of yard space for outdoor parties, a good location in the city, and we had a lot of good times there. It all came to an abrupt end, though, when the landlord decided to sell the property. We were given three months to find a new place to live. Shelly decided to buy a house during that time, and I thought it would be a good idea to do the same.

Of course, I'd never bought a house before, and I didn't really know what I was doing. I was doing okay for myself financially, bringing in about $36,000-$40,000 per year from my job at Comcheq, but I had nothing in savings and very little left out of each paycheck once all of my expenses were accounted for. I also didn't know the first thing about buying houses, but I figured my Realtor could sort that out for me.

The house I ended up buying was a $140,000 bungalow in the Millwoods area of Edmonton. It had a lot of great features: three bedrooms, a finished basement, a huge satellite dish and even a hot tub. My excitement for the place blinded me to some of its flaws, like the fact that the satellite didn't work or the moisture from the hot tub would eventually ruin the basement. It didn't matter. I wanted the house, and I got it, even though I couldn't really afford it at the time. I got my brother to co-sign the title with me, my Realtor helped me find a Cash back Mortgage program, and soon I was a homeowner.

It didn't last long, though. By 2003, I had gone through a lot of powerful life changes, including awakening a passion for travel and a desire to continue my education. Owning a home in Edmonton was no longer part of the plan for my life. I needed money to complete my education and invest in some travel experiences, and selling my home seemed like the obvious solution.

Living in the house for a few years, I had discovered a few things that needed some work. They were small issues that hadn't bothered me while I was living there, but I knew they would need to be changed in order to attract the attention of buyers. I needed to replace the ugly carpeting with laminate flooring, repaint most of the interior and replace most of the trim. The roof also needed some renovations, but I held off and hoped that the house would sell before the snows melted.

That didn't happen. I didn't have time to deal with the furnace or a few other problems, either, which ultimately dropped the value of my home. I ended up selling it for slightly more than I'd paid for it, but I never got to see that money, my down payment or my equity pay down over the years. By the time the lawyer, Realtor and bank walked away with their portions of the sale, I barely walked away with anything at all; I was lucky I didn't lose money in the deal.

I'm not telling you any of this to make you feel sorry for me. I'm telling you because I know that I'm hardly the first person who has experienced this. But I learned from my experience, and I decided to put my knowledge to work. Now, you can learn from my mistakes and profit from my experience.

REASON 2: Sell Your Home for Top Dollar

Regardless of the Market You Get Top Dollar for Your Home

One of the biggest advantages of putting your home up for rent to own is you get the absolute top dollar your home is worth at the time. When it really comes down to it the value assigned to your home is going to be assessed and scrutinized by the bank's appraiser. Each lender has their list of approved appraisers and whatever they come back with is considered the price of the home.

It used to be that appraisers could be swayed one way or another, but all the appraisers I've ever dealt with were strictly by the book and nothing I could say about the property, either positive to get a higher number or negative to get a lower number, would sway their assessment. All the ones I've ever seen rank the property on a number of different criteria with respect to the location, the current sales listed on the MLS, the quality of the interior versus the ones that sold on the MLS, the tax assessment and other factors.

So it really doesn't matter what price your Realtor puts on the home or what price you have on the purchase contract, the bank is only going to value the home based on the assessment. If the purchase price of the home is above the assessed value the bank will only lend based on the assessed value. This is where you separate the shady investors from the investors who truly care about getting people qualified.

For this specific reason I spent thousands of dollars creating new contracts so we could end up selling the home at the assessed value at the time. However, we do have minimums and maximums set in place as well. The minimum protects the homeowner should the market go down during the time of the RTO to own and the maximum protects the tenant buyer should there be an unusual spike in the housing prices during the term of the rent to own.

During the past four years I have received phone calls from individuals who have been in rent to owns with other companies or investors, who were faced with buying a home that was priced $50,000 over the current market value of the home. These companies or investors were sticking to the contract price and trying to force the tenant buyers to come up with an extra $50,000 cash to cover the difference of what the contract price was and what the bank was willing to finance the property for. You can see one of the many ways how investors give rent to own a bad name.

How a Three Year Rent to Own can Net You an Extra $60,000+

I've been talking a lot about the theory behind RTO, but I haven't given you any concrete examples of how well this really works. Let's put some numbers behind it so you can see on paper just how much extra money you can net by renting out your home before its sale.

Let's assume that you have a home worth $300,000. We'll say it's around 1,000 square feet and that it has 3 bedrooms, 1.5 baths, and a 2-car garage. Imagine it's an older, bungalow-style home, but in good condition.

You currently owe $285,000 on the mortgage. The mortgage has just been renewed for another 25 years at a 3.5% interest rate, and you're paying $1,425 a month for it. Once you factor in property taxes and house insurance, you're looking at more like a $1,700 total monthly payment.

In today's rental economy, a house like that would rent for about $1,700 to $1,800 per month. You can probably list it for $309,000 to provide a bit of buffer for negotiations during the sale.

Now, let's compare your options for what you can do with this home: sell it outright through a Realtor, convert it into a rental property or offer it in a rent-to-own agreement.

Traditional Sale

- List the home for $309,000
- Sell it for $300,000
- Pay a 7% commission on the first $100,000 and 3% on the remainder for a total of $13,000 in Realtor fees
- Pay off your remaining mortgage of $285,000

At the end of all that you're left with just $2,000 from the sale of your home. That's hardly enough money to make the sale worthwhile. It's certainly not enough to invest in a new home.

Renting Out the Property

- Charge the high end, or $1,800, for monthly rent
- Budget around $1,800 for annual maintenance, including furnace cleaning, yard upkeep, plumbing, painting and cleaning
- $180 a month for a property manager or the equivalent of your time
- Budget a month or so of vacancy between tenants ($1,700)

Overall, this actually puts you at a net loss of $4,460 each year, and that's assuming that there are no major maintenance issues or catastrophes that come up. If you end up with a bad tenant, you can lose a lot of money on making the home available to rent again.

A 36-Month Rent to Own Agreement

- Receive a $7,500 down payment from the buyer
- Collect $2,050 per month in rent plus option
- Assume a total appreciation of the home over three years to be 5% so your selling price will be $315,000

With those figures in mind, you can see that you can sell the home for $315,000 to your renter at the end of the three years. This automatically makes for an extra $28,000 ($315,000-$287,000) over what you would have net selling the home through a Realtor, but that's not the only profit you'll make. Remember that the buyer has been paying $2050 per month, which is $350 ($2050-1700) cash flow each and every month for you. Over the three-year period that's $12,600 more in your pocket. Lastly, over the three years the tenant buyers is paying down your mortgage each and every month. After three years, the principal is reduced by $22,643, and that amount goes into your pocket as well. So just in cash you have already made $28,000+$12,600+$22,643= $63,243.

Also remember that your renter is responsible for repairs and maintenance on the home. That means that the money you would have lost through a regular property rental gets to stay in your pocket. After three years, that amounts to $13,380 saved. Altogether, then, you managed to make an extra $63,243 and saving $13,380 for a net gain of $76,623 by simply renting out your home for three years and then selling it to the tenant.

Of course, in reality, your own numbers will vary. Your house may be more or less than the calculations offered here, and your expenses might differ. The basic formula behind the rent to own model remains the same, however, and it's always going to be beneficial to you as a homeowner. This is, quite simply, the most effective way to get a great price on your home sale.

Difficult for Many Buyers to Get Financing

As a result of the banks tightening up the lending practices it has made it difficult for many buyers who normally would be approved to obtain financing for a new home. However, regardless of the condition of the market, whether it is going up, down or staying the same, there will always be people with credit issues that need help getting into a mortgage. For the most part, many of these people are good people that just made a bad choice with their credit or fell on some hard times that set them back.

I boil down the countless applications of tenant buyers who seek our assistance and want to get into a rent to own into four basic groups.

1. Contractor – Self-employed or Owns Corporation
2. Currently In bankruptcy or Consumer proposal
3. Good Money and Bad Choices, credit or circumstances
4. Low Income and or bad credit

Contractor, Self-Employed or Owns a Corporation

These individuals are typically some of the best tenant buyers provided their company or profession makes good money. I see so many of these people, especially in Edmonton, who are making $150,000+ per year and typically do one of two things. They are either running as a self-employed person or they are running the income through a corporation. Let me explain what each is doing, why they are doing it and why they can't get approved for a mortgage.

The banks see individuals who are self-employed as pariah. The banks just have no concept of what it really means to be self-employed and how the personal taxes actually work. Let's say for example the self-employed individual is a stay at home mom running a very successful daycare home. Now as a self-employed individual operating their business out of their home they are awarded countless write-offs. Things like a percentage of all household expenses such as mortgage, insurance, utilities, accounting and bookkeeping services, grocery items used for the day home, toys for the daycare home, and a portion of the vehicle, gas, insurance just to name a few deductions.

To show you what I mean, I'm going to run a scenario that compares someone who works for a company and collects a paycheck and a T4 at the end of the year against someone who works for him or herself and claims business expenses on their tax form. First things first, I'm no accountant and all of this is strictly for demonstration purposes. Please consult your accountant to determine what can and can't be written off for your business.

Let's assume for both cases the person makes $72,000 per year. Now if this person had an actual job their T4 would show $72,000 of income, and let's assume they had zero other income, and then their box 150 on their personal Income Tax form would report $72,000. Let's assume basic exemptions for 2012 and run a scenario of how things actually are:

Gross: $72,000

Tax: $1,312.38 per month or $15,748.56 per year

CPP $282.56 per month or $3,390.72 per year

EI $109.80 per month or $1,317.60 per year

Net: $51,543.12

Now, this person has roughly $51,500 to pay for all their living expenses such as mortgage, taxes, insurance, vehicle, gas, toys for their kids, food, and everything else that a typical family would need to spend money on to get by.

If we assume they pay the following expenses:

Mortgage/Rent/Taxes/Insurance = $2,000/month or $24,000 per year

Car and all related expenses: = $750 per month or $9,000 per year

Groceries/meals out = $500 per month or $6,000 per year

Toys/Entertainment = $200 per month or $2,400 per year.

That leaves the mom with $10,100 disposable Income. Now we all know the numbers I suggest are quite low and in most cases there is barely enough money left at the end of the month. But for this example these will do.

Now, individual number 2, instead of working for a company and getting a T4, she is self-employed as a sole proprietor and just runs her business through her personal name. As mentioned, she runs a daycare home out of her house.

Now let's assume individual number 2 runs a successful daycare home and makes a steady income of $6,000 per month that translates to $72,000 per year gross income. Now this lady uses the entire main floor and the basement rec room where the kids are allowed to go. Based on the total square footage of the house she uses 50% of the home to run her daycare home.

Since she uses her car to run for supplies, sometimes pick up and drop off children she calculates that 20% of her vehicle usage is for the business. At the daycare home she offers snacks for the kids and estimates 25% of her groceries go towards snacks for the children, even though her family eats them as well. Lastly, because most of her own children's toys end up being used by the children at the daycare home, she gets to write off 75% of the toys she purchases.

Gross: $72,000

Write Offs for tax purposes:

50% of Rent/Insurance of $2,000/month or $24,000 per year = $12,000

20% of Car and all related expenses of $750 per month or $9,000 per year = $1,800

25% of Groceries/meals out at $500 per month or $6,000 per year = $1,500

75% of Toys/Entertainment at $200 per month or $2,400 per year = $1,800

Taxable Income for Box 150 on Personal Taxes:

$72,000 - $12,000 - $1,800 - $1,500 - $1,800 = $54,900

Based on that the mom would need to pay taxes and CPP to the government:

Taxes owed: $11,000

CPP owed: $2,310

So now we know what the calculations are, let's take a look at the Stay At Home Mom's financial situation.

Gross Income: $72,000

Less Rent: $24,000

Less Car: $9,000

Less Groceries: $6,000

Less Toys: $2,400

Less Taxes: $11,000

Less CPP: $2,310

Total Disposable Income: $17,290

We can see through the example that the Single Mom running a daycare home making $72,000 per year has over 70% more disposable income than an employee working for a corporation making a paycheck. However, in the eyes of the banks the person working for a company gets to use $72,000 of income when qualifying for a house but the single mom only gets to use $54,900 of her income. Even though the single mom, who is self-employed in this example, has more money to service the mortgage and can have more saved for a rainy day, the person who works for a company gets many more advantages with the bank.

Now even if the single mom was running her daycare home through a corporation instead of being a sole proprietor, then her corporation would end up paying less in taxes, but usually when this is the case the person with the corporation does not pay themselves a salary and ends up taking money as shareholder loan or pays themselves dividends to reduce paying personal taxes. Now depending on if the dividends are eligible or other than eligible, you may be recording the income on box 180, which means your box 150 could be blank.

Again, I'm not an accountant, the point I'm trying to prove here is that typically people who are self-employed or contractors generally make good money and have access to additional cash the average employee wouldn't. The issue they usually have is not showing enough money on box 150, and that is what the bank looks at when they are considering a person for a mortgage.

Individuals from this category can be great tenant buyers.

Currently in Bankruptcy or Consumer Proposal

People who are still going through the process of bankruptcy or consumer proposal and have not yet been discharged are typically going to need more than three years for a rent to own. People going through bankruptcy have just eliminated the majority of their debt load and the people who are going through consumer proposal have substantially lowered their monthly outlay of cash to service the debts they had, as they were consolidated and paid back over time at a much lower interest rate. Consumer proposals are typically anywhere from 1-5 years.

Since these individuals are going through these processes getting any new credit is not likely. If the individual is going through bankruptcy typically they are not going to have a down payment, which is something I avoid altogether. I advise these people that as soon as their discharge is complete and they have saved up the minimum down payment required, then they could come back and apply with us again.

If the individual is currently in a consumer proposal, then there is a good chance they may have saved up some money because of the excess cash they have since their debt load has decreased each month. If these people have the down payment and, based on the information from the credit coach and mortgage broker, then typically they are great candidates for longer term rent to owns.

As a rule, these people will need to complete their consumer proposal then spend an additional 2-3 years working with a credit coach to get their credit score to a point they can get into a traditional mortgage. So, for example, if the person has two years left to pay on the consumer proposal then they would need another three years to raise their credit, which means you would need to offer them a five year rent to own.

People in this classification can be hit and miss, which is why I rely heavily on my credit coach and mortgage broker to help me make decisions on whether to accept these people in the program or not.

Good Money and Bad Choices, Credit or Circumstances

Here in Edmonton, and really Alberta as a whole, you really see lots of people who make really great money but made some bad choices when they were younger that affected their credit situation. The people who fall in this category are typically where we like to have our tenant buyers come from. We like to look for the ones who have proven they have already made an effort with their finances by having a larger down payment, those whose lifestyle does not exceed their income and they want to fix their situation and buy a home, but they just don't know how.

Typically these are people in the trades or unions who make a great deal of money, but may have had some challenges when they were getting their tickets and not had enough money to support themselves as they were going through school. This could have led to missed payments, cut off credit cards, or something as simple as switching cell phone companies before the term is up.

You also get a lot of professional people in this group who may have suffered through a divorce that ended up bruising their credit. When it comes to paying the bills during the divorce that both of the individuals are on, neither may end up paying out of spite. This can cause some credit issues once all the dust has settled and the divorce is finalized.

Individuals from this category can be great tenant buyers.

Low Income and or Bad Credit

It is unfortunate, and just as much as I would like to help these people, there is really nothing we can do to help them. Typically the reason they have credit problems is no different than most others, they don't have the income to pay their bills. The difference with the low income individuals is that until they make some changes in their life and put themselves in a position to break out of poverty and make more money, but they just don't make enough to get into a home and qualify.

In a later chapter we will discuss the process for screening the tenant buyers to determine which ones are actually serious about fixing their situation and which ones aren't, which ones will be able to qualify for your home and which ones won't, and some red flags to watch for when you are talking to the individuals directly that will give you cause not to put them in your home.

Helping Yourself Can Help Others

As I mentioned in Chapter 2, I give all the credit of my morality and ethics to my mom and dad. I remember how they were always there to give a helping hand whenever it was needed. That is most likely why I always feel such a strong need to help others, and feel satisfaction when I can see how what I do benefits those I work with.

Now my RTO company gets to help two different sets of people. I am helping sellers who may have otherwise been stuck with a house that they can't sell, or at least not without taking a loss. I am also able to help people improve their lives by being able to see their dream of homeownership come true. People who wouldn't be able to achieve this goal without my help, or the help of others like me.

Of course, I'm not running a charity or non-profit operation. I have to put food on the table and I wouldn't be in this if I wasn't making money. But to do something I enjoy that is also helping other people is a goal many people have, but so few are able to realize.

And I am not the only one who is helping others. As a seller you are helping people who don't qualify for a traditional mortgage achieve their dream of owning a home.

For some people, like me, the ability to help others is important. Knowing that you were able to do something nice for someone else feels good and helps you to feel more satisfied than you would if you sold your home using the traditional method.

Giving People a Step Up

"To know even one life has breathed easier because you have lived. This is to have succeeded." -- Ralph Waldo Emerson

As we discussed in Chapter 1, housing prices are rising faster than income rates in Canada and this is preventing many people from achieving home ownership. People who could graduate from university, get a good job, and then save up for a home are now having their hopes dashed when they realize that the way the economy is today they may not even qualify for a loan.

I am sure you remember what it was like when you fell in love with your home, I know I do. We also already talked about what I had to go through to qualify as a homeowner. If I hadn't been able to buy that home I know how upset I would have been.

That sense of ownership is one some people may never be able to feel if they can't find a home through the rent to own process. While in the traditional market there are more homes than there are buyers, in the rent to own market there are more buyers then there are homes.

I receive requests from so many buyers that, even after they have gone through the qualification process, there are still 30-50 people every month looking for a potential new home just in Edmonton. These are more people than I can place at this point because I only receive one homeowner every month who are looking to use the rent to own option to sell their home. This leaves so many potential tenant buyers waiting for their dream to come true.

And not just for their first home. As with many of us, these tenant buyers may need to purchase another home in the future. By allowing them the time to repair their credit and qualify for a mortgage, you are helping them amend the mistakes of the past. As long as they maintain their good standing with the current mortgage, they can then use the same strategies you are using to purchase another home in the future.

Giving People Their Pride Back

"Give a man a fish, and you feed him for a day; show him how to catch fish, and you feed him for a lifetime."—Anne Isabella Ritche

It is generally believed that the true meaning of this saying is that it is better to teach a person to work than it is to give them a hand-out. This phrase can also be interpreted as when you help a person help themselves you are giving them a gift that will last a lifetime.

And that is exactly what the rent to own process does for tenant buyers. This isn't a handout. So many people come into this program, or ones just like it, thinking that they can just come in, make a few payments, and they will be able to walk into home ownership. That isn't the case. In a later chapter when we discuss qualifying tenant buyers and the documentation process you will see how we set up the tenant buyers for success by providing them the tools, resources and strategies to change their situation and get into homeownership.

Financing Different So Closer to Value of Home

When homeowners sell their home using the traditional method they put their home on the free market where people with the means to buy will make offers to buy the home for what they feel it is worth. Usually what the buyer thinks the home is worth and what the homeowner thinks the home is worth differs until negotiations bring them to a common price they agree upon.

This is the risk homeowners take when they put their home on the market. It isn't the Realtor; the banks or even the homeowner that determines the value of the home; it is the buyer. A home is only worth what someone is willing to pay for it. Of course that is determined by the current market conditions and the competition that home has with the others on the market.

Generally, unless it is a sellers' market, you aren't going to get 100% of your asking price. It is more likely you will get closer to 95% of your asking price or somewhere in between.

Using this system you are typically getting anywhere from 105%-110% of today's value of the home when it sells 2-3 years from now. Not only that, tenant buyers are more than happy to pay for the opportunity to get into home ownership so negotiations typically don't even happen.

Liz N. bought her investment home in an up and coming area. She got a great deal and was able to get it for $250,000 even though the home is worth close to $275,000. Because of the area and the renovations the previous owner was doing prior to her purchasing the home Liz N. is very comfortable setting the purchase price in two years to $300,000. That works out to be 109% of today's value and 120% of her purchase price!

Real estate is one of the most forgiving investments for patient investors. History has shown that property values nearly always go up over time. There may be a few ups and downs, but in the long run, the value will always increase. Depending on the local economy, property values can climb substantially over a period of just a few years.

It's very likely that your home will be worth more in three years than it is today. Even if it hasn't appreciated in value, though, you'll still reap the benefits of mortgage pay-down and monthly cash flow. Additionally, any work you or your tenant buyers put into the property during the rental period will go toward improving the home's value before its sale.

Removing the Fear and Frustration from Home Rentals

Many people shy away from renting out their homes because they do not want to deal with the hassle of being a landlord. What you have to remember, though, is that you will be dealing with a very different demographic when you're offering the property for sale through a rent to own. Renting out a home to an interested buyer is not at all like maintaining a regular rental property.

The people who enter RTO agreements are serious buyers who are looking for an alternative path to home ownership. Unlike more temporary tenants, these renters know that the property they're renting will eventually become theirs. This makes them much more careful and conscientious about what they do while living in the house.

By shifting some of the responsibility for maintenance and repairs to the tenant buyers, you can eliminate your need for a property manager and avoid spending too much time tending to the home. As part of our standard rent to own contracts we make our tenant buyers responsible for all maintenance and repairs under a certain dollar value.

In my Guaranteed Program, where my company leases the home from homeowners like yourself with the option to purchase I will usually complete up to $1,000 in repairs per instance myself. I then turn around and pass that responsibility to the tenant buyers I place in the home on a rent to own arrangement.

Benefits of Offering Your Home as a Rent to Own

When you sell your through a rent to own you have a built-in buyer. This means that you don't have to worry about continuing to market the home or go through a Realtor to locate a final buyer. Let's summarize some of the key benefits of selling your home after renting it out to an interested buyer:

- You can ask for money up-front as a down payment
- The tenant buyer pays down your mortgage with each month's rent check
- The tenant is responsible for maintenance and repairs, relieving you of those costs
- The home, hopefully, will appreciate in value while it's being rented

- Your tenant will have a vested interest in the property
- You receive monthly cash flow until the property sells

You make more money on your home sale, and some of that money goes into your pocket every month. You also help make home ownership a possibility for someone who may otherwise have never been able to purchase your home. It's an ultimate win/win situation, and it's an opportunity that most homeowners would never think to act on.

So far in this section we have talked about accessing equity, a good option if you need to have money to put a down payment on another home or use it for other ways that will help you enter the next chapter in your life. And I have just showed you how you can make $60,000+ or more buy renting to own your home for three years instead of selling it now. We have also talked about how this option is beneficial to buyers who are good people with slight credit problems so that they can get the financing to buy your home at the end of the three year term.

But what about if you are in a situation where you need to pay down your mortgage in order to gain equity or avoid early pay out penalties? Or, even if you are able to come up with a down payment for a new home, how are you going to manage carrying two mortgages while you wait for your home to sell?

In Chapter 7 I will discuss another benefit of the *Rent to Own Revolution*, having someone else pay your mortgage.

Chapter 6

SOMEONE ELSE PAYS YOUR MORTGAGE

"Managing is getting paid for home runs someone else hits."-- **Casey Stengel**

Wouldn't it be nice if someone walked up to you and said, "Don't worry about your mortgage for the next 3 years; I will pay it for you."

You would then be able to focus on other important financial matters. You could pay down your debt, fund your child's education, and even invest your money to increase your income. All of it is possible because someone else is taking the huge burden of a monthly mortgage payment off your plate.

This is in essence what happens when you decide to use the Rent to Own Revolution method to sell your home. And while the idea of someone else paying your mortgage seems like a fantasy, this is how many investment gurus have made their money for years.

This is where the real money is made in real estate. Guys like Trump and Kiyosaki own vast real estate empires where other people pay the mortgage. Having others pay down their mortgage becomes a huge asset to them when it comes time to refinance the property or sell it, such as in the homeowners case. It is like someone putting money in a bank account each and every month that you get to open at a later date. Every month that goes by the amount that gets put into the bank account gets larger. This reason is one that most people forget about, because they don't see the immediate results.

Traditional Pay Down vs. Rent to Own

In Chapter 4 we briefly touched on the idea that sometimes people need to sell their home before they have had a chance to build equity. People often try to plan out their lives, but circumstances can change and where they saw themselves in 5 or 10 years is no longer possible. Whether their lives are changing for the better or for worse, their current home is no longer a part of this new life plan.

This can become a major issue if the homeowner has only purchased the home within the last few years. As homeowners pay their mortgage a portion goes towards the principle amount borrowed, while a larger portion goes towards paying down the interest. You see, banks are smart, they want to get their money as quickly as they can, which is why such a large percentage of the payment is interest at the beginning.

This means that the homeowner hasn't been able to pay down the principle of the loan so that he or she can begin to build equity. And without that equity, the homeowner may not be able to qualify for another mortgage to purchase a new home.

Even if the homeowner is able to delay purchasing a new home until they sold the old home they still may be facing a mortgage prepayment charge. So, you may be lucky enough to find a buyer, but you will walk away with nothing, or even have to pay money out of your pocket because you are selling your home early.

Mortgage Prepayment Charges

Do you understand all of the charges and penalties that are involved if you pay off a closed mortgage early? If, so congratulations for most homeowners don't. If you don't, it's okay. Closed mortgages are confusing and banks make all of the charges hard to determine. The Department of Finance has been urging banks to agree to a code of conduct that includes providing calculators online for homeowners to use when trying to determine penalties.

Many banks, including ING Direct, HSBC, the Royal Bank and TD Canada Trust have taken the Department of Finance's suggestion to heart. They include mortgage calculators so that homeowners can see what it will cost them if they decide pay off their mortgage early. Not all banks do this, however, and non-lenders don't do it with their closed mortgages either.

The Financial Consumer Agency of Canada is taking steps to make banks reveal how they calculate the prepayment charges. The Consumer Agency is also encouraging fairer penalties for early payoff.

Even with the risk of penalties that are difficult to determine, most buyers prefer a closed or limited open mortgage to an open mortgage. This is because of the lower rate that can equate to a significant savings over a traditional mortgage.

When you purchase a home you don't look at the fact that you will be selling your house 2 or 3 years from now. You look at the fact that you will own your home for a long period of time. In your mind you will own the home long enough that you will have to refinance your mortgage at the end of the 5 years that is standard for long-term, closed mortgages.

And these closed mortgages do offer you the ability to make additional payments so that you prepay the mortgage without a penalty. It is just that the lender places limits on how much you can pay and how often you can make a payment.

Here is an example offered by the <u>Financial Consumer Agency of Canada</u>:

Example

- John received a raise, which allowed him to save $15,000.
- He decides to use it to make a prepayment on his mortgage at the beginning of the second year of his term.
- However, his mortgage lender limits prepayments to a maximum of 10% of the principal.
- John wants to know whether he can make that large a prepayment, and if so, how much sooner he will be able to pay off his mortgage as a result.

If John has a $150,000 25-year mortgage with a 5.45% interest rate, and the lender allows a lump-sum payment limit of 10% of the principle a year, the pay down would look like this:

Over the mortgage period	No prepayment	Prepayment (beginning of second year)
Prepayment lump sum	-	$15,000
Principal	$150,000	$150,000
Interest payments	$123,368	$90,168
Total amount paid	$273,368	$240,168
Interest savings	-	$33,200
Years to pay off	25	20.7

John would be able to pay $33,000.00 less interest during that 25-year term and pay the mortgage off 4 years earlier. That is the way banks want you to pay off your mortgage, because, even though you may be paying it off early, they are making their money.

The truth of the matter is that most long-term, fixed rate mortgages terminate early. Over 25% of these closed mortgages terminate mid-way through the five-year term. When you payoff these mortgages early, what you are paying is the interest differential. This is what the banks charge you to make up the difference from what you promised to pay and what the bank would earn from a current mortgage.

Borrowers don't always know how much they will be charged when they pay off their mortgage early. But the payment can be huge and homeowners are often shocked. Even with the steps the Department of Finance and Financial Consumer Agency have taken to make banking practices more transparent in terms of closed mortgages, there is still information that isn't disclosed. That information can make a difference between what you think you will pay based on the mortgage calculator and what the banks say you owe after you have paid off the mortgage.

There really isn't anything the homeowners can do to change the way the banks structure mortgages, but what they can do is have someone else pay the mortgage so when it comes time to sell they get to recover the equity. The longer you can have someone in your home paying down the mortgage the more money you will make at the end when it is sold.

Rent to own Pay Down

For Chaang Y. this was one of the factors that went into his decision to put his home into this system. He calculated that by just having someone else pay the mortgage for the next 3 years he would walk away with an additional $12,000 in his pocket. When you add in the fact he wasn't going to have to pay a Realtor approximately $10,000, doesn't have to pay a mortgage penalty for getting out early, and getting full market price for his home, Chaang Y. get's to walk away with at least $22,000 more in his pocket. If you recall, selling today would have cost Chaang Y. money.

Typically 95% of the tenant buyers that get into these arrangements require 3 years or less to turn their situation around. There are some who do require longer terms of 5-7 years, depending upon their situation. With this system we put the tenant buyers through a stringent screening process using mortgage brokers and credit coaches so you know exactly how many years of mortgage pay down you will benefit from with each tenant buyer.

If you recall I started just after the crash in the housing market of 2007/8. I was meeting with countless homeowners about leasing their homes and having the option to purchase the homes at the end of the term. Well I was meeting with so many homeowners who bought at the absolute peak of the market and now needed to do something with their home, as they couldn't stay in it any longer. They knew by renting the home they were going to suffer a loss each month, but realized they needed time for the mortgage to get paid down and hopefully the market to adjust and start creeping upwards.

Well fortunately for the homeowners their mortgage did get paid down because in Edmonton there was little to no growth during the past 5 years. I think back to all the kitchen tables I sat at in 2009/2010 and listened to the homeowners tell me the market was going to rebound with appreciation like during the boom, so why should they give me the option on their home for today's value. I'm sure most of those owners, if they could do it all over again, would have agreed to work with me. At least by dealing with me they would not have had to deal with the hassles of renting their property to tenants.

One of the properties I took over in my first 6 months doing this business was a half duplex in the community of Rutherford in Edmonton. The owner purchased this home at the very peak of the market for over $400,000 and at the time I did my analysis it was worth maybe $340,000-$350,000. The owner did some calculations and based on where his mortgage was at he needed 4 years before the mortgage would be paid down to $355,000, so that is the price we settled upon.

As I am sitting here writing this book I recently had the conversation with the owner of the home because the 4 years are going to expire this October 2013. This particular property had 2 different groups start the rent to own then with one month's notice, just left. Because they knew the option money they paid was non-refundable there was no questions on their part, their situations changed and they just couldn't stay there any more. Now, I currently have renters in the home who have expressed interest in buying the home next year.

So when I talked with the owner a couple of weeks ago it came as a shock to him that I wasn't going to buy the home. Once he got over the shock I explained the situation. Even though his mortgage got paid down to the $355,000 range, the value of the property was still only around the $340,000-

350,000 range. My purchase price with him was higher than it was worth. Even if I had a tenant buyer in the home I would have been requesting either more time, because the home was not worth my price with him, or I would have needed him to drop the price by 5% in order to put the deal through.

The reason I'm brining up this particular case is to demonstrate the saying Real Estate is forgiving, you just need time. In this case there just hasn't been enough time pass for it to be forgiven yet. For this owner, I feel 2 more years with this property will allow him to sell the property and walk away breaking even or actually putting money in his pocket. Oh, and of course I did offer to extend for another year as the couple in the home wants to buy the property and would pay Fair Market Value at the time, plus I would need to structure the paperwork to build up their 5% down payment during that time. So it has been left in the owner's hands to see what he wants to do.

An Example of Mortgage Pay down

Just to give you an idea of how you can determine what your mortgage pay down would be on your home I'm going to walk you through an example so you can get the idea. After I walk you through this example, I'm going to tie it into the interest you would pay when using RRSP's to get some of the equity out of your home.

For this example we are going back to the example we were using in Chapter 4. If you recall we refinanced that home so there was a $240,000 mortgage on the house. We are going to assume we amortized it over 25 years and got an interest rate of 3.5%.

The table shows cumulative totals

I used the iPhone App called Morgulator+ to get the figures in this table

	Year 1	Year 2	Year 3	Year 4	Year 5
Starting Balance	$240,000	$233,863.29	$227,509.92	$220,932.23	$214,122.31
Monthly Payment	$1,198.25	$1,198.25	$1,198.25	$1,198.25	$1,198.25
Total Paid	$14,378.99	$28,757.97	$43,136.96	$57,515.94	$71,894.92
Interest Paid	$8,242.28	$16,267.89	$24,069.19	$31,638.25	$38,966.88
Equity Pay Down	$6,136.71	$12,490.08	$19,067.77	$25,877.69	$32,928.04
Ending Balance	$233,863.29	$227,509.92	$220,932.23	$214,122.31	$207,071.96

You can see that at the end of 5 years the mortgage balance is down to $207,071.96 from $240,000 for total equity pay down over the 5 years of $32,928.04. Now if you assumed this period of time was from 2008 to 2013, where there was not much appreciation in Edmonton, and the home was still just worth $300,000 then just by owning this home and having someone else pay down the mortgage you can see you would have made $32,928.04.

What you have to realize is the first 5-10 years of any mortgage is where you pay the most amount of interest. So if you recently refinanced your home at 15-20 years because you already paid 5-10 years on the home then the rate in which the principle gets paid down increases dramatically. For example, the balance of the mortgage at the end of the 10th year would have been $167,905.88, which means the mortgage would have gone down a total of $72,094.12.

This is where the power of real estate lies. When you have someone else pay down the mortgage over time you can capitalize on the equity pay down after you sell your home. Just think about it for a minute, you got the equity out of the house at the very beginning using the strategies and techniques from the earlier chapter, you still own the house and can expect a payday in the future of between $19,067.77 and $32,928.04, depending on the length of the rent to own term you have with the person in the home. Remember, this also assumes zero appreciation for the term of the rent to own, which is not that common.

Now let's put this mortgage pay down in context with the example from Chapter 4. First I will run through the example as if you did not use anyone else's RRSP's to take out equity, then we will run the same scenario as if you used $30,000 of RRSP's at 10% simple interest over the time of the rent to own.

Scenario 1 - 3 Year Rent to Own, No RRSP's used.

If you recall from Chapter 4 this was the situation on the home after you refinanced it and pulled out $30,000 Cash.

Current Value: $300,000
Mortgage Value: $240,000
Mortgage as % of Value: 80%
Equity: $60,000
Equity as % of Value: 20%
CASH IN HAND: $30,000

After Rent to Own is signed

Future Selling Price: $315,000
Option for Future Purchase: $15,000
Balance Due Upon Sale: $300,000
Mortgage Value: $240,000
Mortgage as % of Balance Due Upon Sale: 80%
Equity: $60,000
Equity as % of Balance Due Upon Sale: 20%
CASH IN HAND: $45,000

For this example I am only focusing on the amount of money you will make from the sale of the home at the end of the term. I am not looking at the Cash Flow, which will come in a future chapter.

For your home I am going to structure a simple 3-year rent to own on the home, with the future purchase price of the home set for $315,000. Now if you recall, the tenant buyer came into the rent to own with $15,000 down up front and in this example they are not paying any additional money monthly to go towards the future purchase of the home. In this example, at the end of three years they will need to come up with $300,000 to buy the home, which they will get from the bank in the form of a mortgage.

At the end of the 3 years the tenant gets a mortgage from the bank for $300,000 that goes to your lawyer to pay out the mortgage on your home. When that happens the lawyer pays the bank $220,932.23, which leaves you a cheque of $79,067.77. If you recall, you had $60,000 of equity still in the home so that means you made $19,067.77 when the house sold. Also, don't forget you received $15,000 up front from the tenant buyer and there would have been cash flow, which we will touch on in a later chapter.

Based on this information, you have recovered the entire $60,000 made $15,000+$19,067.77 or $34,067.77 and saved yourself $13,000 in Realtor commissions. Now remember, we still have monthly cash flow to consider, which will all come together in a later chapter.

Scenario 2 - 3 Year Rent to Own, RRSP's used.

If you recall from Chapter 4 this was the situation on the home after you refinanced your home then found someone with $30,000 to register on the house as a mortgage.

After RRSP Mortgage is registered

Future Selling Price: $315,000
Option for Future Purchase: $15,000
Balance Due Upon Sale: $300,000
1st Mortgage Value: $240,000
RRSP Mortgage Value: $30,000
Mortgages as % of Balance Due Upon Sale: 90%
Equity: $30,000
Equity as % of Balance Due Upon Sale: 10%

CASH IN HAND: $75,000

For this example we have negotiated to pay simple interest of 10% per year on the RRSP value. To calculate the RRSP due at the end of the 3 years let's take a look at the table.

	Year 1	Year 2	Year 3
Starting Balance	$30,000	$33,000	$36,300
10% Interest	$3,000	$3,300	$3,630
Ending Balance	$33,000	$36,300	$39,930

You can see at the end of the 3 years you will need to pay back the $30,000 to the RRSP and the $9,930 of interest back into the RRSP account when the home is sold. This is why I caution against using this strategy. So let's take a look at the numbers now.

As you know, you already received $75,000 of your equity upfront, leaving $30,000 of equity in the home.

So just like in Scenario 1 the tenant buyer needs to finance $300,000 through the bank so your lawyer receives a cheque for $300,000 but needs to pay out all the mortgages. Let's see how much you will make at the end of the deal. Remember, you got your money out up front so everything else is a bonus.

Amount Received from Lawyer: $300,000
Payout of 1st Mortgage: $220,932.23
Payout of RRSP 2nd Mortgage: $39,930.00
Total of Payouts: $260,862.23
Cheque from Lawyer: $39,137.77
Equity return: $30,000.00
Profit made on sale: $9,137.77

There are several things to notice and think about here.

First thing to notice is when you started you had a 1st mortgage of $240,000 and a 2nd of $30,000 for $270,000. At the end of the 3 years the payout was $260,862.23 which means even with the interest paid to the RRSP account the payout was still less then the starting value. The mortgage percentage dropped from 90% loan to value down to 87%, so even through though the home did not appreciate in value the payout still reduced. This is extremely important to understand. You never want to put yourself in a position where you have the home financed more than 90% and you want the combined mortgages to be lower at the end of the rent to own term then when you started.

Second thing to take into consideration is you received $75,000 of your equity out of the home before you even started, then received another $30,000 at the end when the home sold, plus $9,137.77. You were able to take your $75,000 of equity out up front and use it to invest in other properties, and by selling during the rent to own you get out another $30,000 of equity and $9,137.77 of mortgage pay down. Compared to if you just sold the home and took your $75,000 and walked away, here you got the $75,000 out upfront and was able to walk away with another $39,137.77 at the end of the sale.

Third, we haven't even looked at how much money you will make from cash flow monthly. We will look at this in a future chapter.

Lastly, something you will need to consider is it worth paying the $9,930 in interest over the 3 years to get $30,000 out up front. Now I'm not saying that you have to pay 10% interest, I'm sure there are many people out there making 2-3% interest on their RRSP's who would be happy making 5-8%. The benefit of the RRSP mortgage is you get to negotiate the rate you pay.

These options are still preferable to losing money when you sell your home using a Realtor and facing prepayment penalties from the greedy banking system. They are also preferable to renting your home to someone who isn't going to buy it at the end of a 3-year lease. Not only will you be getting money in your pocket at the end of the sale, you won't be losing money because you have to make expensive repairs on the home.

With the rent to own system, the tenant buyer pays for the repairs. We will be covering this reason to rent to own your home in Chapter 7.

Chapter 7

CONTROLLING YOUR COSTS

"Life for rent means that my life isn't really my own, I only rented it for a while, but if I don't manage to buy it, to own it, then nothing of what I think is mine is really mine."--Dido Armstrong

Throughout this book we have been talking about not selling your home, but instead helping a great family get into homeownership while at the same time making and keeping more of the money from the sale of your home. One of the best ways to keep more of your money is to control your expenses.

Typically one of the hardest things to do is get a homeowner to consider their home as a business. Usually homeowners have such an emotional attachment to the home things can tend to get clouded. Hopefully with this chapter I can turn off your homeowner switch and turn on your internal CEO switch, so you start thinking of your home as your company and you are the CEO in charge.

REASON 4: Someone Else Pays the Repairs

As the CEO it is your job to maximize revenue and minimize expenditures. Let's take a look at what some of those expenditures are and how best you can reduce those line items in your expense sheet.

The first item we are going to look at is one of the largest, that being the expense of a Realtor. If you are using or considering using a traditional realtor for the sale of your home you can expect to part with a considerable amount of your equity. If you recall the example back in Chapter 4 when we were looking at getting your equity out of the home we looked at what it would cost you to sell your home. To refresh your memory here is the example from Chapter 4.

Now for our example we need to sell the home. In this example we are going to have you use a traditional realtor who is amazing at his/her job and gets you almost full price for your home. Here is how things would go with the sale of the home.

Selling Price: $298,000
Commission (7% on first $100k and 3% on the rest) $12,940
Net Selling Price: $285,060

As you can see, selling your home through a realtor would cost you $12,940, which would go directly in the expense column of your Income Statement and would reduce your net income. Basically it is going to cost you a lot of your equity to sell your home and you would have no future income, you would be selling your company.

Rental Expenses

As homeowners venture into the landlord arena they usually don't take into account the amount of expenses they will soon be faced with. It isn't just the expenses that come along with owning a home but when you throw in the human element, such as tenants, you never know what you are going to end up paying for.

Getting the late night calls when the toilet is overflowing, midnight moves, damage to the property, vacancies, non-payment of rent and the endless excuses homeowners face when turning their home into a traditional rental. It is for these reasons homeowners shy away from becoming landlords.

In order to look at the other expense items we first need to take a look at typical and traditional expenses landlords are faced with when they rent out their homes. This is going to be a quick course on landlording101.

One of the first things you need to consider and budget for when renting out your home is vacancy. Now what I was taught by my mentor Ross, who has been investing for over 30 years, is that if your home is a single family residence, whether it is a house, condo, duplex, or townhouse you should always budget for 1 ½ months of vacancy. This doesn't mean it is going to be vacant for that long, but you should budget for that length of time. I also realize there are those who do real estate investing who say that is absurd, so to try and eliminate conflict I am just going to use one month for my example.

If you were to rent out your $300,000 home in a decent area of Edmonton you would probably get $1700 rent for the property right now. So we need to budget for $1700 of lost income each year. Basically, when one-tenant leaves you need to get into the property and have it professionally cleaned, repaint the property and see to any minor or even major repairs. Now this usually isn't going to get done between noon on the last day of the month, which is when the leaving tenant must be out of the home, and noon on the first day of the month when the new tenant is scheduled to move into the home. As a result there is going to be a month where you don't have any income to cover the mortgage, taxes, insurance, condo fees etc. so we will need to expect to cover those items. Instead of getting into too much detail with actual costs we will just use the $1700 as the expense item.

The next expense to look at would be your maintenance and repairs on the property. This will really depend on the current condition of the home as well as the type of tenants you have living in the home. Unless you have been tracking the expenses you have paid out on your home to cover the day to day items that need to be fixed, getting the gutters cleaned, having the furnace cleaned, any landscaping that needs attention, fixing or repairing holes, etc. I typically budget one months' worth of rent. For maintenance and repairs we are also going to budget $1700 per year.

For most homeowners they have no desire to actually manage their rental properties and like the idea of passing that task off to a property manager. For those who do manage their own rental properties it takes up time, energy and resources to look after the home. They need to deal with maintenance and repairs, running to the bank for deposits, checking on the home, accounting and so much more. Looking after these things, your time, gas, etc. is worth just as much as it would be if you were paying someone else to do it for you. When it comes to this expense 10% of the rent value is standard. That equates to $170 per month or $2040 per year.

Typically when you rent out your home you have the tenants pay for the utilities. However when the home is vacant the utilities fall on the shoulders of you, the homeowner. Since we have budgeted for one month of vacancy in the home we would need to budget for one month of utility costs such as heat, water, electricity and anything else. Obviously depending on the month of the year it was vacant would really determine how much the expense would be. I'm sure if you went through your bills you could get a good average, but for our example we are going to estimate $300 for utility expenses for the month.

When you have one tenant move out and another tenant move in you should always get the locks changed or re-keyed. You never know how many people have keys from the previous tenant living in the home. Depending on how many locks you have in your home and the type of locks will really dictate how much you want to budget. For our example we are going to assume there are two doorknobs and deadbolts that need to be changed and each basic set will generally run approximately $75. For our expense budget we are going to want to allocate $150 per year towards security.

Another item that most investors don't budget for but has been a recent issue in Edmonton recently is pest control. There has been a large outbreak of bed bugs in the Edmonton area over the last year. Many investors did not budget for this expense and were left completely off guard. For this expense we are going to budget $300 per year for pest control.

The last item we are going to account for is actually accounting. For most, running a rental business is just that, a business. For your average homeowner they aren't going to know what they can write off and what they can't. It is best to pay an accountant to look after your taxes when dealing with having a rental property. For this we are going to budget $500 per year as an expense.

Now let's add up the budgeted expenses for the year and see how much we end up with.

Vacancy:	$1,700
Repairs and Maintenance:	$1,700
Prop. Mgt/Time Value	$2,040
Utilities:	$ 300
Security:	$ 150
Pest Control	$ 300
Accounting	$ 500
Total	$6,690

When we take the total allotted expenses for the year and get a monthly amount we can see that we need to budget $557.50 each month. So if we are treating this like a business your income is $1,700 for the month and your mortgage taxes and insurance come to a total of $1450 per month. At this point, what most people do is say well I'm making $1,700-

$1,450 = $250 per month cash flow. But what they haven't accounted for yet was the other estimated expenses, which total $557.50 per month. This puts the homeowner in a negative cash flow position.

Don't get me wrong, I'm not sitting here saying that every year you are going to actually have all of those expenses, but what I am saying is that you better budget for them because there are many times when homeowners and landlords get less than desirable people in their properties and end up paying or losing this much or more. These are just great rules of thumb when it comes to budgeting and looking at renting your property.

The real reason for walking you through this exercise is I needed to make you fully aware of what kinds of expenses you should be looking at and approximate values you should be looking at since this chapter is about controlling your expenses.

Tenant Buyer Pays Many Expenses

One of the best parts when it comes to dealing with a rent to own, or a tenant who is wanting to buy the home at the end of the term is they will care for the property more so than the average tenant. But just like my mentor Ross says, you still want them to treat the home like it is yours, because you are still the one on title. You never know how people live. You also get the benefit of transferring a lot of the expenses over to the tenant buyer. Let's take a look at the list a little more in detail.

The first one is the obvious big one, the realtor commissions. If you are doing the RTO yourself using the *Rent to Own Revolution* program you are not going to need a realtor at all, you are only going to need your lawyer to close on the sale of your home, just like you would if you sold the home in the traditional manner. It is much cheaper to get your lawyer to fill in the sales contract at the end of the rent to own then to have a salesperson. This will end up saving you about $12,940. (One thing to note is there are other things you need to take into consideration when closing on the sale of the rent to own, which we will discuss in the documentation chapter.)

I'm going to address vacancy and utilities together. It is true the person can end up leaving or not paying during the term or the rent to own, however you should have collected at least three months' worth of Non-Refundable Option money plus a security deposit. Typically you have upwards of four months' worth of rent to offset any non-payment or if they give notice and leave, however the security deposit must be handled according to the rules of the Landlord and Tenant Act for your area. Vacancy is a rarity in rent to own, but it can happen. In the rent to own scenario you are better positioned financially should it happen.

Repairs for Rent to Own

Repairs and maintenance in a RTO scenario are different as well. Typically in the agreement with the tenant buyers you make them responsible for all repairs and maintenance up to $500 or $1,000 per instance. This puts the onus on the tenant buyer for all the little things around the home and you then become responsible for the larger items such as the furnace, hot water tank, roof etc. If those things are in good shape and wouldn't need to be replaced you may be able to go the entire 2-3 years without spending a cent for repairs. I have had several home owners that I've worked with who have never had to spend a single dime on their property in the three years they had it in the rent to own program.

Property management responsibilities are dramatically decreased when you are dealing with rent to own. Because the tenants are responsible for the repairs and maintenance you don't get the calls to fix the clogged toilet or service the dishwasher that isn't working. As a result, there are times when you only need to visit the home four times a year to do your quarterly inspections on the property. Other than that you rarely ever hear from the tenant buyers and most of your time is spent ensuring the appropriate documentation is in order for the rent to own.

This can be time consuming, and at the same time it can be very low maintenance. Because of the screening practices we use, the agreements we have with the tenants who want to become homeowners we spend very little time managing the rentals. We do our quarterly home inspections to ensure the home is being maintained in an appropriate fashion but for the most part our processes and systems have decreased the amount of time being spent managing the properties. Having systems, processes and procedures in place can eliminate the amount of time you spend.

Right now, when my company rents a home from a homeowner we will pay for all the repairs and maintenance up to $1000 per instance. I think there was two times when I went to the homeowner for repairs. Once was when there was a crack in the foundation and it was causing water damage in the basement. The owner had to get it repaired at his expense. The other was for a variety of things after years of neglect: painting, dish washer, wiring and a few others. Other than those two instances, the homeowners love just collecting their cheques and never hearing about problems that come up.

There can be times as well when things happen in the person's life that causes financial problems with the tenant buyer and you need to get involved regularly because of late or non-payment of rent. These don't happen as often with people in rent to owns, especially the ones you have put through the screening process I will teach you in a later chapter. To say these don't arise would be untrue. It can get to the point where it is just like a rental.

With our guaranteed program we guarantee to return the home in the same condition less normal wear and tear, if our tenant buyers don't purchase the home and or leave. One such home was a side by side duplex in Calder, Edmonton Ab. For the most part we had good tenants in the property. They always paid their rent, looked after the home and even did improvements at their own expense like fence, yard, interior etc. There was a young couple living on one side and his mother living on the other side. The home was under one title and the young couple entered into the rent to own.

Well after 3.5 years they young couple decided they did not want to buy that duplex as they didn't want the hassles of having roommates or their mother living beside them anymore. They decided to walk away from their option money. When they left the mother was none too happy. She decided to take everything she put into the place with her. We had to go in and buy a washer and dryer, some closet doors, some door knobs, replace the hood fan, and the kitchen sink faucet. We also fill countless screw holes in the walls from shelves, TV's, etc. Then we had to get a dump bin to empty the garage and yard. It ended up costing us almost $3,000 and three days but we honored our agreement with the owner. We handed back the home in the same condition less normal wear and tear. All the homeowner had to do was get the interior painted. We did the majority of the prep work for the painters by filling all the holes. Obviously the home owner didn't like the fact the tenant buyers went the entire time and didn't buy the home, but he did like that for the 3.5 years he didn't have to sink one cent into the home for repairs and maintenance, had his rent paid on time each month and never had to worry about vacancies or paying a property manager. During the four years there was zero appreciation of the home, and actually it slightly went down in value as a result of the market in Edmonton during those years, but the owner did benefit from close to $40,000 in mortgage pay down and zero expenses. If he hadn't gotten himself into financial trouble to the tune of

$60,000 to some high interest lenders he would have entered into another rent to own with our company. Unfortunately, he needed to sell the house to pay off his outstanding debts.

When these instances do arise your effort can increase, especially when it comes to posting notices on the home for non-payment of rent, 24 hour notices to enter the property, documentation should you need to take them to the landlord and tenancy board. We will discuss this more in the chapter on documentation.

Pest Control and Locks

Just like all the other expenses, pest control is the responsibility of the tenant buyer, so unless they leave the property and you are stuck with a pest issue it is their responsibility to deal with the situation.

Changing the locks is something you are going to want to do if the tenant buyer leaves. During the regular course of the RTO you wouldn't need to account for this expense.

Liz and Chang

Liz N. didn't want to turn her next home into a traditional rental. She didn't want to have to deal with all the problems she has been faced with in the past. Those problems included just about every one listed earlier in this chapter.

Liz N. realized she didn't want just a tenant; she wanted someone who had a vested interest in living in her home, someone who was going to be responsible for the care and upkeep of the home because they were eventually going to own the home. For those reasons Liz N. decided to put her home in this system and have the tenant buyers responsible for all repairs and maintenance up to $1500 per instance. That would cover everything in the home, unless the furnace was to go. Since a brand-new one was just installed it is unlikely she will have spent a cent on the property for the next two years.

Similarly for Chaang Y., using this system he was able to have his property renovated at the tenant's expense prior to them moving into the property. Chaang Y. was able to structure this in lieu of taking a large down payment up front. What is important to note is that the tenants weren't allowed to move in until the renovations were complete and qualified contractors had to be used. No do it yourselfers allowed.

When having the tenant buyers get the property renovated there is a better chance they are going to care for the home and purchase the home at the end of the term. Chaang Y. also made the tenant buyers responsible for up to $1,000 or repairs and maintenance per instance.

Another major expense is the selling expense when using a realtor. Typically you will pay 7% of the first $100,000 and 3% of the remaining amount of the home. There are numerous discount brokerages popping up, along with do it yourself systems such as ComFree and The PropertyGuys.

Although the do it yourself systems are usually around the $1000 price point if you are going with the best package, there is still a lot of work to be done on the homeowners part and it can still take time to sell the home. Homeowners can be sitting on the property for months before they even get an offer.

Rules of Thumb

Since I talked about rules of thumb earlier when it came to renting out your property I'm going to touch on a couple of rules of thumb when it comes to rent to own and how much of an initial option (down payment) you accept from the tenant buyer. Typically you want between 2-3% of the purchase price or three months' worth of rent.

If you recall from earlier examples we were going to rent to own the home for $315,000, which means 2% of that value is $6,300 while 3% is $9,450 and three months' rent comes to $5,100. So based on the two rules of thumb you can make $5,100 your minimum required option payment or $6,300 as the minimum. A couple things to keep in mind is the person is also going to be paying a security deposit of $1,700, one month's rent of $1,700 and a monthly option amount which will depend on how you structure the rent to own.

In this particular example here is what I would want. I want enough to cover my estimated yearly budgeted expenses, which if you recall was $6,690. I would actually round that up to be a minimum of $7,500, which is about 2.5% of the purchase price. I would also want the $1,700 security and the $1,700 rent plus the first month's option amount of $250. The grand total I would want from the tenant buyer up front to get into your home would be $10,650.

Doing it this way, you know you have collected enough money up front to cover your estimated expenses should things go south on your rent to own and you need to cover your expenses. You will notice that you are also collecting an additional $250 per month, which adds up to $3,000 per year over and above what you would collect from rent. First, we will talk about cash flow in the next chapter and second, if you haven't already done so send in your receipt for this book to receipts@RentToOwnRevolution.com and you will get access to the training videos that will walk you through calculating how you make your money turning your home into a rent to own. You will also have access to worksheets, calculators, and some documents. It is a $497 value absolutely free just for buying this book.

Remember, before you put anyone in your home you put them through a stringent qualification process that you will also find in the video training program that weeds out the undesirables or those who's finances don't measure up for the value of your home. Using my process the tenant buyers you select will truly want to get into home ownership and you are going to be the person to help them. The process walks you through outlining all the expectations and clearly lays out their responsibilities when they are in your home.

Getting back to you being the CEO of your own home who has the responsibility of increasing revenue and controlling expenses, hopefully I was able to help you understand how turning your home into a rent to own accomplishes both. First, you have no realtor fees, second the tenant buyer typically pays the repairs and maintenance and pests, which reduces your amount of time and work. These longer-term arrangements also mean there are fewer chances of vacancy, utilities, and security.

You have also collected a large non-refundable option consideration, hopefully equal to or greater than the total budget for your yearly repairs. If anything goes wrong you have already collected money to cover the issues that may come up. You also have a security deposit to cover any repairs or maintenance that needs to get done should the tenants leave the home without buying. Not only have you collected money up front but you are also getting more money each and every month.

If you were a CEO of any fortune 500 company and you managed to decrease expenditures and increase revenue as you did for your own home by turning it into a rent to own you would be receiving some serious stock options and bonuses for your performance!

These are all great reasons to join the *Rent to Own Revolution* instead of resorting to traditional methods of selling your home or renting it. But, I am sure many of you are wondering what the month to month figures look like. I have touched on this subject a few times over the last three chapters, but I won't keep you waiting any longer. In Chapter 8 we will take a look at a payment schedule so that you get to see the type of money you can make with this process.

Chapter 8

CASH FLOW IS KING

"There's lots of things that can be solved with cash."--Danny Boyle

The fifth and final reason to turn your home into a rent to own is one of the most significant, and that is that cash flow is king! Cash flow, in case you aren't aware, refers to the amount of money you have left over each and every month after all the expenses are accounted for.

If you recall back in Chapter 7 we talked about controlling your expenses. We looked at some of the monthly expenses associated with your traditional rentals. These same expenses you may actually have with a rent to own as well, depending on your tenant buyer. As long as you did your due diligence screening the tenant buyer and nothing changes in their life circumstances then you should not have a problem with the tenants paying and looking after the property.

Cash flow is very deceiving to many as they only look at the gross figures and fail to take into consideration actual or budgeted expenses for the property. For the layperson just renting out their home getting $1700 per month in rent while their mortgage taxes and insurance are $1450 per month they feel they are making $250 per month. After reading Chapter 7, I really hope you don't think that this is the case. For most people the actual cash flow will be somewhere between +$250 per month and -$557.50 (taken from the calculation in Chapter 7), depending on the quality of the individuals in the home.

Truly, this is not that much different when it comes to rent to own, however you have transferred the responsibility onto the tenant to look after the repairs and maintenance as well as have a lease term of around three years. Now, depending on the individuals, they may or may not do the repairs and maintenance, and they may or may not leave or stop paying rent. The bonus with the rent to own is that you should have received enough money from the tenant buyers up front to cover the costs of a typical year's worth of expenses should something happen.

Again, going back to Chapter 7 we calculated the estimated yearly costs for renting out the home was to be $6690 per year and you determined the least you would take for an upfrontnon-refundable Option Consideration Payment (down payment) was going to be $7500. This means if it came right down to it you have enough money to cover the typical expenses you would incur by just renting out your home upfront and in advance.

REASON 5: Money Doesn't Lie

Getting Extra Money Each Month

Now with your typical RTO situation the tenant buyer comes into the agreement with a non-refundable option consideration payment (down payment) and agree to pay rent plus an additional amount over and above rent that would get credited towards their down payment if and only if they exercise their option to purchase the home at the end of the rent to own term.

As we touched on in the previous chapter we would be looking to have a total monthly payment of $250 over and above the $1700 rent for a total of $1950 per month and if you recall we had a monthly expense of $1450 for mortgage, taxes and insurance. This leaves a gross cash flow of $500 per month. From Chapter 7 we discussed controlling expenses and passing on the repairs and maintenance to the tenant buyers, which will leave you with close to the $500 per month cash flow.

Now I have been doing rent to owns since 2009 and I can confidently say that even when I've had tenants leave the property part way through the rent to own term, the houses were always left in good condition, with the most expensive home costing me approximately $3000 to get show ready again. That was the home we discussed in Chapter 7, but before you say $3,000 is a lot let me tell you how much I made on this particular home.

This was the very first home I put on a rent to own. I worked with the homeowners and leased their property, which was a side-by-side duplex under one title, for $2600 per month. I had lease option contracts with them for three years. In September 2009 I had a young couple, Ryan and Crystal, get into the RTO with Ryan's mom living in the other side of the duplex. To get into the property Ryan put $5,000 down and agreed to pay $3,200 per month, giving me a gross cash flow of $600 per month.

During the three years both groups did a pretty good job at maintaining the home, doing some work outside at their own expense, updating some of the inside in some areas and leaving other parts as they were. When the end of the term came due Ryan and Crystal decided they did not want the property because they didn't want to have anyone, especially their mother, living beside them. They ended up just walking away at the end and moving on to going out and buying a small single family home, using their RRSP as down payment.

So let's take a look at the financials on this property. They rented the home for 36 months giving me a cash flow of $600 per month for a total of $21,600 cash flow over the course of three years. They also gave me $5,000 up front for a grand total of $26,600. Now, take into account the $3,000 I had to spend getting the place back into its original condition, less normal wear and tear, and I still profited $23,600. You can see that when it was all said and done, I netted my $600 per month cash flow and $2,000 from the initial option money. This is the power of turning your home into a RTO and having someone else responsible for the repairs and maintenance.

I'm going to share another example of a property I leased from a homeowner and turned into a rent to own. The home was a 2007 built ½ duplex with a two car attached garage. This particular property I had a 4-year term on, which I was paying the owner $1300 per month and I ended up getting a family into the home originally with $5,000 down and $1800 per month, which gave me $500 per month cash flow.

Unfortunately this family had a life event that put them in a position where they had to leave the home just before two years were up, which meant I had just over two years left with my lease option with the owner. Again, this family had done a fairly good job keeping up the condition of the home but in order to get it show ready I would need to repaint and clean the carpets and furnace. I ended up spending about $2,000 getting it ready to rent to own again and ended up paying for one month of rent plus utilities. All in total I paid $3500 before I had someone ready to move in.

A 30-something single contractor, Gord, was my next tenant buyer who came into the rent to own with $7500 down and was paying $2000 per month for a 2-year rent to own term. Gord was in the property for just over a year when his company took an awful hit. He was doing a job and the plumber he hired told Gord he had insurance, but Gord didn't check his paperwork. The plumbing job went bad and left Gord with a terrible mess, which as the general contractor he was responsible for. This was going to cost Gord tens of thousands of dollars to fix and repair. Because of that Gord had to leave the property and go move in with relatives so he could spend all his money to fix the home he was working on.

Now when Gord left the house he did an amazing job, he basically got it show ready for me by repainting, carpet cleaning the works. This time I didn't have to pay to get the home fixed up, but I did have to pay for one months' worth of rent as Gord couldn't pay for the last month he stayed there. I did get some amazing renters into the home as soon as the home was finished for the last year of my lease with the owner. The tenants were paying $1650 per month and they were amazing tenants who never required anything from me during the term of the lease. I was able to get the home ready to hand back to the owner at the end of the lease with just some basic cleaning, which cost me $250.

Now, let's take a look at how I did on this home and what my cash flow ended up being when I factored in all the expenses I had to pay out:

Money Out: $3,500 for 1st tenant buyers, $1,300 to owner for Gord's unpaid Rent, $250 for clean up at the end. Grand Total is $5,050

Option Money In: $5,000 plus $7,500 = $12,500

Less money out: $ 5,050

Total $ 7,450

Cash Flow: 24 months at $500 per month = $12,000

             12 months at $700 per month = $ 8,400

             12 months at $350 per month = $ 4,200

Total Cash Flow
$24,600 or $512,50 per month

Total Profit: $7,450 + $24,600 = $32,050

You can see, in this example where I had three different groups of people come through the property because of circumstances or changes in their lives that I still had $7,450 left over from the upfront non-refundable option money, averaged $512.50 per month in cash flow and made a total profit of $32,050.

I wanted to use these real life examples to show you what kind of tenant buyers you can get in your homes. For the most part, if you are using the screening process I'm going to discuss in the next chapter then even if the individuals end up leaving the home and don't purchase the property you should be left with all your cash flow as typically in my experience the amount of work and clean up needed is typically less than the upfront non-refundable option payment you accepted at the beginning.

Back to the Example

Getting back to our example where you were collecting $1950 per month after $7,000 non-refundable option payment (down payment) and paying out $1450 per month you should easily be able to net your $500 per month cash flow.

Just think what an extra $500, $600 or even $700 per month could do for you without having to deal with the issues, maintenance and repairs you would with your typical tenants.

Remember my investor friend Liz N, the real estate investor with a couple of rental properties? She wanted to get into some more real estate but did not want to deal with any more issues that come with your typical tenants. Let me review the scenario with you and then we can discuss her cash flow on this property.

Liz decided to buy a home and put it into this rent to own and received a $15,000 non-refundable payment from the tenants before they moved in and is making $750 per month in cash flow each and every month. Her tenants are responsible for all repairs under $1500 per instance, so unless something major happens to the property Liz will never spend another cent on the property. In two years when her tenants buy her home Liz will walk away with over $40,000 profit just from the appreciation and mortgage pay down. The total profit over the two-year period will be $73,000.

In one year Liz will have $9,000 of cash flow on top of the $15,000 she received down on the property, so if anything did happen and the tenant had to leave and Liz had to get the home show ready she would have lots of cash in which to make it happen. Now Liz, just like me, usually inspects the properties on a quarterly basis just to ensure the home is being kept up to the standards we expect.

Having cash flow of $500-750 or more for 2-3 years is a very compelling argument to keep your home and turn it into a RTO rather than just sell it out right or rent it then sell it.

Now you have a better understanding of the 5 major benefits of turning your home into a rent to own:

- Access to Equity
- Selling Your Home for Top Dollar
- Someone Else Pays the Mortgage
- Someone Else Covers Repairs
- Money Doesn't Lie

In Chapter 4 we discussed how this option will allow you to access your equity. This can be important if you are looking at needing a down payment so that you can obtain a mortgage for a second home.

When you try to sell a home through a Realtor, you will have to sell your home in order to gain access to your equity. The amount you receive using this method is often reduced because you need to pay Realty commissions and you may be subject to mortgage prepayment penalties. After these costs are deducted, you can lose all of your equity and may have to pay some of the expenses out of your pocket.

With the rent to own method you have the ability to keep more of your equity and gain access to it before the home is sold. With a rent to own, you can refinance your home and receive some of the equity as cash. Then you can receive a non-refundable down payment from the tenant buyer as a condition for allowing them to rent the home for three years and then purchasing it. The amount you receive is typically 2%-5%. If you need more cash on hand then you can require a 5% down payment to help you with your own financial situation.

If you need a large down payment for a second home but refinancing the home and receiving a down payment from the tenant buyer isn't enough, you can seek an RRSP mortgage to help with the difference.

An arm's length RRSP mortgage benefits both parties. The investor will receive accrued interest as well as the original note. The homeowner is able to negotiate the terms of the mortgage with the investor to free up funds while receiving optimal repayment terms.

While having access to equity shouldn't be the main reason to look at rent to own, it is a benefit that traditional options of selling your home can't give you. A second benefit to turning your home into a rent to own was covered in Chapter 5.

When you use the *Rent to Own Revolution* method you are able to sell your home for top dollar. In Chapter 5 we took a look at what happened when I sold my first home. After paying commissions, fees and penalties I wasn't able to receive the money I was looking for to cover the costs of going back to university. This story is the same for so many homeowners out there, especially in today's market.

But in the realm of RTO it is always a seller's market. Because there are more people who are looking at trying to do rent to own and not enough homeowners, you can set an asking price that will allow you to receive more money than you would in a traditional sales situation.

Another contributing factor to obtaining top dollar for your home is the fact that you are setting a sales price based on an estimate of what the home will be worth three years in the future. Hopefully the house will appreciate during that time so you will be able to sell the home for more money in the future than you would if you sold it on today's market.

Even if housing values in your area don't appreciate during that three year period you are still looking at the ability to receive a down payment, money from the tenant buyer's monthly rental payments, and the final sales price of the home when the tenant buyer obtains a mortgage and pays you the balance of the asking price.

In a traditional real estate sales situation the buyer will often try to negotiate a lower selling price for your home. You will also have the realtor pressuring you to accept the deal because they want to make their money and move on to the next listing. Finally you will have to deal with the housing market as it is, instead of being able to wait for the conditions to improve.

If you have an upside mortgage, or you are in a closed mortgage, you have to sell your home with the knowledge that you could walk away with nothing. Not only does rent to own save you from losing money you also have the benefit of someone else paying down your mortgage during that 3-year term.

In Chapter 6 we looked at how a tenant buyer's down payment and monthly rental payments will help you pay down your mortgage. This will help you gain access to more equity and avoid prepayment penalties when you pay off your mortgage. We also took a look at how little of our payments go to the principal during the initial years of a long-term mortgage. The majority of each payment goes to interest first, so after 5-10 years you haven't been able to make an impact on the principal of the loan.

With rent to own you have options available to you to get out from under the burden of an upside down mortgage. You also have the ability to buy a second home before you are able to sell your first home. In this market, so many people are stuck because they are unable to sell their home and they don't have the money they need to buy a second home.

Not only are you able to free up the money you need to purchase a second home and earn some money every month from your first home, you are also able to keep more money in your pocket during the 3-year rental agreement. This is because the tenant buyer covers the majority of home expenses. This is the topic that we covered in Chapter 7.

Chapter 7 took a look at the expenses you would need to cover when you rent your home without offering the option for the tenant to buy it after three years. When you include the costs of vacancies, utilities and repairs, many homeowners lose money when they rent their home. When you add in factors such as pest control, damage to the home and tenants who leave without paying rent, you can see why many people don't like to become landlords.

The situation is different with rent to own. Many of the expenses the landlord needs to pay in a traditional rental situation are covered by the tenant buyer in a rent to own agreement. Other costs rarely occur. For example, when you offer the option of renting to own the home you rarely need to deal with vacancies. The tenant buyers are motivated to buy the home and don't want to lose the money they invested in the program with the down payment, security and monthly rental payments.

Tenant buyers usually take good care of the home while they are renting it. This will be their home in three years, so they take care of it as though it was theirs now. Tenants in standard rental agreements don't have this type of incentive to take care of the home.

In most cases the tenant buyer will also take care of repairs that are needed during the three year rental agreement. Unless the cost of the repair exceeds $1,000, most rent to own contracts stipulate that the tenant is responsible for replacing appliances, fixing a leaky roof, or clearing a clogged drain. Many homeowners are able to rent their home for three years and sell it without having to cover the costs of any repairs.

Not only do they cover repairs, many tenant buyers will make renovations on the property during the rental term. They are looking at the property as their future home; therefore the tenants will be inspired to make the home better before they purchase it. And any renovations they make during that time will increase the value of the home when it comes time for the house to be sold.

Finally, we have the benefit of cash flow, the last reason why you should turn your home into a rent to own. This is what we covered in this chapter, and I explained to you how receiving a down payment will be able to compensate for expenses you will need to pay for a rent to own. You will also be able to receive a higher rental payment than you would with a standard tenant. This extra money will not only allow you to put money towards your mortgage but also have funds for expenses at your new home if you need it.

With all of the benefits you receive from the RTO method why would you ever resort to the traditional avenues to sell your home? Now all you need to do is find out how you go about turning your home into a rent to own.

That is what we will be covering in Section 3. You will get to see the different steps you will need to successfully turn your home into a rent to own. We will then provide you with additional information on these steps so that you will gain a better understanding of all of the tasks you will need to complete for each stage of the process.

We will review the type of research you will need to conduct in order to calculate the asking price, down payment and rental payment. Then I will show you how to advertise your RTO the right way in order to attract the right type of tenant buyer and avoid any misconceptions due to the bad publicity rent to owns have received.

First we will take a look at how to pre-qualify buyers. As we have discussed in the first two sections, many hard working and diligent people are no longer able to qualify for a traditional mortgage without a little help. Other individuals may have had a problem in the past, but they have turned their life around and are now looking for a second chance with a new home.

These are the type of tenant buyers you want for your home, but how do you recognize them when you find them? And how do you separate these worthy tenant buyers from the people who will never be able to resolve their credit issues or can't afford to purchase the home at the end of a 3-year term?

I will you show you our process so that you can see what my company does beforehand when we qualify tenant buyers to make sure we will be able to place them in homes. This will be able to shed light on the process you will want to put in place.

The last step we will look at in this process are the contracts you will need to make your rent to own successful. I have mentioned several times in this book how important the paperwork will be to you during this process. I have spent a lot of time and effort to create contracts for my rent to owns so I know all the pitfalls that await you if you don't have the right documents and create a paper trail.

Section 3 How to Rent to Own a Home

Chapter 9

RENT TO OWN STEPS PART ONE

"A leader is one who knows the way, goes the way, and shows the way."--John C. Maxwell

In Part 3 we get to the heart of the matter: the steps you will need to turn your home into a rent to own. These steps are:

- Research
- Calculations
- Advertising
- Screening Applicants
- Contracts

There is a lot of information to cover and some of it is complex. To help make things easier for you I am going to divide these steps between two chapters. In this chapter we will review the first three steps research, calculations and advertising. In Chapter 10 I will discuss screening applicants and contracts.

From the homeowner side there are many things that need to be taken into consideration. Not only do you need contracts specific to this type transaction that are designed to protect yourself, you need to understand the Landlord and Tenancy Act, you need to have a mortgage broker that knows how to present the information in the correct manner to the lenders so they recognize the sale, you need a credit coach that is going to work with the individuals to ensure they are doing everything necessary to be able to qualify at the end of the term. Lastly, it is important you take any and all necessary steps to ensure the individuals entering into the agreement with you understand what they are getting into. These are the reasons it is best if you work with a company that specializes in all the above.

When I first started into this type of business I was educated and mentored by an individual who had successfully transacted hundreds of lease options over his 30-year investing career. There were times he had to go to court because things didn't work out the way they were planned and every time he lost he did one thing, he asked the judge what he could have done differently to get a favorable result. Each time this happened he had his team of lawyers change his contracts or he changed his process. Through his teachings to me since my beginning I have adopted all of his contracts, lawyers and processes, as well have added some extra ones of my own to protect the company and the homeowners I represent. The education and mentorship alone cost me $40,000, not to mention what I have spent on lawyers and systems to ensure my homeowners are protected when they work with our company.

This is not meant to scare you, but to impress upon you the importance, like anything, to hire specialists. Our company has been working with home owners since 2009 and to provide the homeowners like yourself even more assurances and guarantees, we have put together a program where we will be your tenants, renting your property for three years and have the option to purchase the home at the end.

(This is right from my ad)

OUR COMPANY DOES THE FOLLOWING:
- Pay your rent every month GUARANTEED!
- Put quality tenants into your property
- Provide a long-term lease agreement (from 1-5 years)
- Handle all the management responsibilities
- Handle all the maintenance and repairs up to $500 per instance.
- Provide interior insurance
- Buy your house at the end of the lease term at a GUARANTEED Price
- Close quickly

Obviously for our company to assume the majority of the risks by offering this program there needs to be a financial benefit to us. I'm going to be crystal clear on this, as I don't want people wasting my valuable time, if you are one of the greedy homeowner types and want it all, don't contact me about my services. Greedy homeowners want everything, which leaves nothing for me.... so why would I want to waste my time?

If you are like most of the homeowners who are ok making considerably more money than you would by just selling or renting on your own then selling, are ok not having to do any work or shell out any money at all while the home is being rented, feel there is a value to what my company offers, my services, my expertise, and you are ok with the fact that my company makes money helping you then I would love to help.

Just as every home, townhouse, condo, etc. is different in some way, so are the scenarios with the homeowners. Homeowners have different needs, and until I know your needs it is hard for me to know the best way to help. Maybe you need some money now, maybe you need some extra money each month, maybe your house needs some renovations and you can't afford it…. there are so many different scenarios.

Ioffersolutions Real Estate Services Inc. has become the Trusted Authority when it comes to helping home owners like yourselves get more money for your home, while at the same time helping other individuals get into home ownership. We have built a reputation of honesty, trust, integrity, and acting with morals and ethics by educating both the homeowners and the potential owners about the risks and advantages of our program.

Whether you chose to work with us or take part in the revolution on your own, you still need to have a thorough understanding of the process. We will start with research, the essential step needed in order to create the calculations for the rental agreement and purchasing costs.

A Step-by-Step Guide to Renting to Own Your Own Home

Let's take a look at how to turn your home into a rent to own.

Step 1: Research: Before you can calculate how much you are going to make by turning your home into a RTO you first must know a few things about your home and your market.

The first thing you need to know is the value of your home. There are typically two ways you can get this value.

First, you can ask a Realtor to give you a comparative market analysis. This is free and you can get it by contacting a Realtor and letting them know you are considering selling your home but want to know how much homes like yours are selling for and the length of time on market.

Second, you can contact a registered house appraiser to get an appraised value of your home today. They take into consideration the current sales of other homes, tax assessment, upgrades your home may have, the location and some other criteria. Getting an appraisal can usually run approximately $250-400 depending on the company.

The second thing you need to know is the rental market for properties just like yours in the area. Finding a value for your home takes a little bit of website surfing and a few phone calls. Websites like kijiji.ca, craigslist.com and rentboard.ca are just a few websites where you will find available rentals.

Try to find properties in your area to determine what fair market rent may be for your home.

Another quick way to find the market rent for a property just like yours is to call property management companies to see if they have anything available to rent similar to your property and the amount of rent. These companies are usually professionals and are constantly on top of the market knowing the rental prices for various areas.

The third and final thing you will need to know is the past performance of your area as well as the expected future outlook. This information, as well as a great deal more, can be found on the CHMC website at www.cmhc.ca. When on the CMHC website you are looking for the Housing Market Outlook - Canada and Major Centres. The web address to take you directly to that area of the website is

https://www03.cmhc-schl.gc.ca/catalog/productList.cfm?cat=63&lang=en&fr=1372960372250

This will give you a good indication what has taken place in your market place over the past 2-3 years and what is expected in the next 1-2 years ahead. This information can give you a good indication what you can expect as far as appreciation for your home.

For example in Edmonton we have the following statistics:

2010 Housing prices dropped -0.8%

2011 Housing prices rose 0.9%

2012 Housing prices rose 0.9%

2013 Housing prices forecast to rise 1.5%

2014 Housing prices forecast to rise 2%

Now you have all the financial information you will need in order to determine the financial components needed when turning your home into a rent to own.

Step 2: Calculations: Now that you have done all the research required to find the value of your home today, what the fair market rent would be as well as the performance of the market in the past as well as the near future, it is time for you to set the numbers for turning your home into a rent to own.

Calculate the End Price

To calculate the end purchase price you will need to take today's value of the home and multiply it for every year of the term. For example let's say that you were going to turn your home into a rent to own at the very beginning of 2013. You would take today's value of the home and multiply it by the appreciation factor of 2013 and add the two values together. You then take that number and multiply it by the appreciation factor of 2014 and add them together. Finally you would do it one last time for 2015. But as you can see, CMHC did not give a value for 2015 so the best thing to do is to follow the trend over the past five years.

You can see that in 2010 there was a slight drop in house prices, then there was a modest gain of .9% in 2011. The following year there was another gain of 0.9%, followed by 1.5% and 2%. Since 2012 we can see the housing market has increased by .6% (1.5-.9) and .5% (2-1.5) so it would be a safe bet that we could increase 2015 by .5% over 2014. This would give us a value of 2.5% for 2015. This kind or reasoning doesn't always work, because it is so hard to predict long term appreciation as there are so many factors that need to be taken into consideration.

Now, let's take a look at our $300,000 home and see what the end price would be if we set up a 3-year rent to own.

Current Value: $300,000

Year 1 Appreciation: $300,000 x 1.5% = $4,500

Value after year 1: $300,000 + $4,500 = $304,500

Year 2 Appreciation: $304,500 x 2% = $6,090

Value after year 2: $304,500 + $6,090 = $310,590

Year 3 Appreciation: $310,590 x 2.5% = $7,764.75

Value after year 3: $310,590 + $7,764.75 = $318,354.75

So for our example the home valued at $300,000 today we would estimate it to be valued at $318,354.75 at the end of the RTO. For me, however, I wouldn't use such an exact number, I would round it up to the nearest thousand or maybe even nearest ten thousand. For example I would advertise this rent to own with an end price of $319,000 or $320,000.

Currently, the way I have my contracts structured I actually have two prices on them. The first being a maximum value of the home, the second being a minimum value of the home with the actual price being set by the appraiser of my choosing at the time. For our example let's set the maximum value of $320,000 and the minimum value of $300,000. At the end of the three years the lender sends in the appraiser to value the home, so let's look at a few different scenarios.

Scenario 1: The appraisal comes back at $318,750. If this were to be the case the actual price of the home becomes $318,750.

Scenario 2: The appraisal comes back at $325,000. If this happens the contract price reverts to the maximum value of the contract, which is $320,000.

Scenario 3: The appraisal comes back at $285,000. If this were to be the case the selling price would revert to the minimum price of $300,000.

For scenario 1 it is straight forward, the price falls between the min and max values so we accept the appraised price. For scenario 2 the appraised value fell outside the maximum value so based on the contracts we revert to the maximum value. I know what you are thinking, why don't we jack up the price of the maximum value so we get to sell it for whatever it appraises at?

First, I don't object to having the maximum value slightly higher then your estimated appraised value just in case the market rises higher then expected, however you need to be able to justify the price to the home owner. If you tell them the maximum price is $400,000 at the end of the three years on a $300,000 home it makes absolutely no sense. If you thought to yourself, well the average per year now is 2% so I think I want to use an average factor of 3%-4% then it would be acceptable in my eyes. Anyone who set's the increase over 5% in a market when the current average is only 2% is really just out there to take people's money in my opinion.

The second reason, which we will touch on more when we get into screening the tenant buyers, is that the people you put into the home must qualify to buy a home that has a value equal to or greater than the maximum value. So again, if you set the maximum price of your $300,000 home at $400,000, when it should be around $320,000, then you need to make sure you have someone who qualifies for a mortgage of $400,000. I guess, in reality, if you are marking up the end price to $400,000 then you probably aren't worried about the people qualifying because you are just out there to screw people over anyway and part of the group giving this business a bad name. It is for this exact reason I had new contracts created so the true value of the home based on the appraisal is what the tenant buyer is ultimately going to pay.

Now let's take a look at scenario 3. If you were to sell your home today you could have sold it for $300,000. You decided not to sell it, but rather help someone else out and get him or her into a home.

For this reason we set the minimum value of the home at today's fair market value. It is my opinion that you should at least get what the home is worth today; however, where this doesn't work well is when the rent to own is entered into at the peak of a market and there is a dramatic drop in the housing price and it then stays flat for a few years. This happened to many people who entered into a RTO during the peak of 2007 in Alberta and when it was time the buy the home the minimum value was still not close to what the home was valued at in 2007.

A good rule of thumb is that if there has been 2-3 years straight of amazing appreciation and you are in a market where the values are jumping up by thousands of dollars every single month and there are bidding wars on houses, my opinion is to throw up a For Sale by owner sign on the lawn fast and put it up for sale on the internet. There is a good chance you will also get a bidding war on your home and sell it for top dollar and maybe even above market value at the time. I say you should do this because I am fully aware that real estate runs in cycles, and whenever you have increases like that and a buying frenzy it is always followed by a crash.

Calculate the Initial and Monthly Option Payments

Ok, so now we have the purchase price figured out, now we need to calculate how much of an initial option consideration (down payment) the tenant buyer will need to get into your home. In order to do this you need to know that the government requires home buyers to have a minimum of 5% down payment in order to qualify for a mortgage. Yes, there are some places where you may be able to still get zero percent but those are for people with exceptional credit, not ones who have just fixed their credit.

So for a tenant buyer to be able to qualify for a mortgage at the end of the RTO they are going to need to have 5% of the purchase price saved or paid to you already as their down payment. The way I structure the pricing, with the minimum and maximum you will always want to calculate 5% of the maximum value. This way you are assured they have enough built up, and in cases where the value is at the minimum value they will actually have more than 5% built up. Let's take a look at our example.

Based on the maximum price of $320,000 the tenant buyer would need 5% of a down payment, or $320,000 x 5% = $16,000. So by the end of the 3-year rent to own the tenant buyer would need to have given you $16,000 towards the purchase of your home. Depending on how you structure your rent to own you could take all the money up front then charge them rent for three years and they can buy it at the end, or like in most cases you charge them 2-3% of the purchase price up front then they pay the difference over the course of the term. Let's see how that would work.

Max Purchase Price: $320,000

2 % Upfront Option: $320,000 x 2% = $6,400

3% Upfront Option: $320,000 x 3% = $9,600

For our example you know you should not accept any less than between $6,400 to $9,600 for an upfront option payment. For our example we are going to use a value of $7,500 as the minimum value we will accept. So you determine that $7,500 is the minimum upfront option payment you will accept, which leaves $8,500 to be paid over the course of the rent to own. The $8,500 would come in the form of monthly option payments that get paid as a separate payment over and above the rent or lease payment. To determine how much they need to pay, let's take the remaining amount to be paid, $8,500 and divide it by the number of months in the term of the rent to own. In our case we are doing a 3-year rent to own so that would equal 36 months.

$8,500/36 months = $236.11 per month

For me, I like to round this number up to the nearest $25 so I would make their monthly option payment $250 per month. So when it comes time for the tenant buyer to buy the home you can show the lenders, through the help of your mortgage broker, the tenant buyers paid you $7,500 up front and $250 per month for 36 months for a grand total option payment of $16,500. As per the contracts, when the tenant buyers actually purchase the property you then convert the option money to their down payment on the purchase of the home.

The sales contract would look something like this:

Initial Down Payment:	$7,500
Other Down Payment:	$9,000
Balance Owing:	$303,500
Purchase price	$320,000

From this you can see they have paid you $7,500 upfront, $9,000 over the 3 years and the balance due to you at the sale is $303,500 for a total purchase price of $320,000. The $303,500 is the amount of a mortgage they need to get from a lender in order to buy the home. Provided everything went well through the 3 years and they worked with the credit coach, which we touch on later in this chapter and the next, there shouldn't be an issue getting qualified.

Calculate the Rent Amount

When it comes to calculating the rent I take a couple of things into consideration. First, what is fair market rent for this house today? I believe in the previous chapters we indicated it was $1700 per month. Second, I like to look at what the actual costs of the home will be when the homeowner buys the house. Based on them financing $303,500 at the end, using todays benchmark interest rate of 5.24% over 25 years we calculate the monthly mortgage payment would be $1806.86.

Now we know when it comes to a house there is more than just the mortgage, there is also the taxes and insurance. If we assume the taxes and insurance are another $250 per month combined then the tenant buyer would be looking at $1806.86 + $250 = $2056.86 per month as a grand total for their payment.

I like to look at all this information and ensure I'm setting the tenant buyer up for success. I want to make sure that the value they are paying me today is close to what they would be paying me in the future when it is time to qualify. So based on the estimate future total payment of $2056.86 I am going to use $2050. Now out of the $2050 we have to allocate $250 towards their option payment, which leaves $1800.

So based on my calculations, if I were to charge the tenant buyers $1800 for rent plus the $250 for monthly option payment they would be paying $2050, which is roughly what they would be paying for their mortgage, taxes and insurance when it is time to buy the home, using the benchmark interest rate at the time set by the banks. By using this model you can see you have put a considerable amount of thought into ensuring you are setting your tenant buyer up for success.

For some who do this business they would charge their costs on the property plus the option payment, which if you recall was $1450 per month cost for mortgage, taxes and insurance. If you took that value and added the $250 you end up with a payment of $1700, which is today's fair market rent. Many would want to charge just the $1700 per month and credit the $250 towards their option payment. Not only does this leave money on the table that you could be putting in your pocket each and every month but you have not done the tenant buyer any service. They get used to paying $1700 then when they go to buy all of a sudden they are paying $250 more per month, it can be a shock. I like to train the tenant buyers right from the very beginning to pay what they would be paying in the future. If they can't pay it now how can we expect them to pay it when it is time to qualify?

For this segment you will need to refer to the accompanying tools you will find when you send in your receipt to receipts@renttoownrevolution.com and gain access to the complete video training and resources for turning your home into a rent to own.

Step 3: Market Your Home for Rent to Own: Once you have worked through the financial components of the rent to own it is time to start the marketing process.

The first thing to know is the majority of people start their searches on line, so having a good Internet presence for your rent to own is crucial. There are various sites where you can market your home for free including Kijiji and Craigslist. Both of these sites have areas specific for real estate and if you don't mind re-posting your ad once a day you can be seen by hundreds to thousands of people each and every day.

You can also post your home on rental sites such as www.RentBoard.ca or for sale by owner sites, such as www.ForSaleByOwner.ca where you can even pay extra to get it listed on the MLS website. The more exposure you are able to create for your home the easier it is to attract interest and get a qualified tenant buyer.

Using this system automatically gets your home listed on one of the most recognized and respected rent to own websites in the country. At www.ioffersolutions.com and www.ioffersolutions.ca, along with all their city websites, they attract numerous tenant buyers each day applying to get into one of the rent to own homes through their program. Not only do they have new people coming to the site daily but also have one of the largest databases of people looking to get into a rent to own home they can market to directly.

The second thing to remember is people usually drive the neighborhoods they want to live in, so signage is important. You want to have a sign that catches their attention and has a call to action to get more information. Having them call your phone is not what you want to happen. You will spend more time trying to explain how RTO works and get a lot of people without money contacting you. You want to provide people who are interested with as much info as you can without ever talking to them initially.

You can do this by having them call a number that goes directly to a message where you can leave the details of the property, the rent to own information, where they can go to download a brochure, when you are having an open house, how they can get more information and how they can apply. You can ask them to leave their name and number if they would like a call back. This will eliminate you constantly trying to explain how the rent to own program works and only those interested after hearing all the details will leave their name and number.

The *Rent to Own Revolution* System will give you a word for word script you can use for your message. Not only that, we can provide you with a dedicated phone number that will track things like the person's phone number, it will give you a system where anyone driving by can scan the QR code or text to the number to automatically receive all the details about the home, the rent to own, the application as well as the application process. You can even have instant text messages be sent to all those interested advising them of any open house you are going to have. The system will be completely automated and set up for you!

For an example of a truly automated system that does everything for you, including booking the showings for you, test it out. The house even has it's very own website. The following example is for the FREE Rent to Own Revolution Member's area, however the exact same system that takes people to a website or delivers automated responses is used for capturing contact information for the people interested in your home.

TEXT NAME AND EMAIL TO
780-800-7464

OR Scan the QR code

OR Visit
http://0s4.com/r/RTOMA

This is the best method to use in order to find potential tenant buyers who are interested in renting a home for three years and then buying it. But are they capable following through on the contract? In Chapter 10 I will go over the screening process you will need to use in order to find qualified tenant buyers. I will also explain the contracts and paperwork you will need to have in order to protect you, your home and the tenants during this process.

Chapter 10

RENT TO OWN STEPS PART TWO

"For a successful revolution it is not enough that there is discontent. What is required is a profound and thorough conviction of the justice, necessity and importance of political and social rights".--B. R. Ambedkar

In Chapter 9 we reviewed the first three steps that are involved with turning your home into a rent to own: research, calculations and advertising. I explained where you need to go to collect the data you need in order to determine a purchase price for your home, an upfront option and the monthly rental payments. We discussed how to try to see into the future in order to determine a sale price that won't be too high or too low at the end of the 3-year term. I also showed you how to determine a fair rental for the home so that you are covering your expenses and making sure the tenants can afford to continue to make monthly payments after they have purchased the home and are paying a mortgage.

In Chapter 10 we will be looking at screening the tenant buyer and the contracts you will need for the RTO process. To give you an overview of what we will be covering here I will explain to you how my company screens the tenant buyers for our program.

Our qualifying process is second to none and one of the best programs in the country, partnering with a mortgage brokerage that specializes in rent to owns and a Certified Credit Coaching company that aims to help the individuals going through our program succeed. We set our future homeowners up for Success right from the very beginning.

INFO FROM WEBSITE EXPLAINING OUR SCREENING PROCESS

On helping people who are in trouble, It is important for us to create a win-win situation When it comes to Rent to Owns it is important to partner yourself with a company that has a system in place designed to set you up for success from the very beginning. At ioffersolutions Real Estate Services Inc. we pride ourselves on our processes, procedures and the businesses we have partnered with to ensure each family coming through our program has all the tools, resources and support to succeed from day one!

Everything starts with the initial phone call, response to an internet ad, visiting one of our Rent to Own homes or filling in one of the forms on our website. When you initiate contact with us we aim to follow up with you within 24-48 hours, depending on the day of the week. During our call or email we gather some basic information about your situation, what kind of home you are looking for, what area you wish to live in and what your budget is for your new home. Just like a mortgage broker it is important for us to have a general idea how much you make per year so we can manage your expectations. There are so many people who contact us making $30,000-$40,000 per year, with a monthly budget under $1000 per month everything included and want a $400,000 home. That just isn't realistic and we do our best to manage your expectations.

Once we have gathered some of the basic information and answered your questions regarding the Rent to Own program we then forward you a copy of our application. At this point nothing happens until we receive the completed application from you. When that happens we forward the application to our mortgage broker and credit coaches for their review. The mortgage broker will let us know the maximum monthly mortgage payment, as well as the maximum purchase price of a home you would qualify for based on your income and expense levels today. The mortgage broker also gives us a rough idea how long it would take, given your current credit situation, for you to qualify for a mortgage.

After the credit coach has received your application you can expect to get a call wanting to set up a meeting with you to discuss your current credit situation. It is MANDATORY for all our Rent to Own clients to meet with the credit coach and work with them during the term of the Rent to Own. During the meeting the credit coach will evaluate your current situation, assess what can be done with your current debt if there is any, what needs to be done to fix, raise or create credit and determine the time frame required to get you where you are today to where you need to be in order for the mortgage broker to secure you a mortgage. The coaches then set out a step by step instruction plan that will get your credit score to the point where our mortgage broker can get your qualified. The coaches then schedule meetings with you on a quarterly basis to review what you were supposed to do and what you accomplished.

Upon completing your initial meeting with the credit coaches and having your information reviewed by the mortgage broker we now know the maximum home value, what your maximum monthly payment can be and how long it will take before you will qualify with a bank. With this information and your commitment to meet with the credit coaches quarterly we can put you into one of our rent to own homes knowing we have done everything possible to ensure you are on the path to rent to own success!!

When you are looking at potential tenant buyers you need to follow the same process. You will want to make sure the individuals who want to be eligible for your rent to own have a thorough understanding of what they will need to do in order to meet your qualifications.

Step 4: Screening the Tenant Buyer: Without a doubt this is the most crucial piece of the entire *Rent to Own Revolution* program. You want to make sure you have done everything in your power to set them up for success right from the very beginning.

As a result of the lack of information around reputable RTO programs you will get people from all walks of life thinking they are going to be able to get into your home and pay less than they would if they were just renting. The key for you is to set the expectations right up front by letting the potential tenant buyers know how much income they would need to make to qualify for your home as well as the process they will need to go through in order to be considered.

There are two major pieces of information you need to consider before even thinking of putting someone in your home on a rent to own basis. The first thing is their income or ability to service the mortgage based on their current level of income. The second is their credit situation and how long they need to repair their credit before they can qualify with a traditional lender. Knowing these two pieces of information are crucial to your success and setting up a win-win situation.

Mortgage Broker

When it comes to qualifying an individual based on their income you will want to use the same formulas the banks use, as they eventually need to qualify with the banks. The banks typically use two formulas. One formula looks at 32% of the combined household income to go towards the mortgage, taxes for the property. The second formula ensures the applicant has a total of 40% of the household income to service all their debts.

For example, a family that makes $60,000 gross income (before taxes and deductions) would be able to support payments yearly payments totaling $60,000 x .32 = $19,200, which translates to a monthly payment of $21,000/12= $1,750 per month. If, for example, the home has property taxes of $100 per month and we allocate $100 per month for heat it leaves $1,550 to go towards the mortgage payment.

To determine how much of a home you can get for $1,550 per month it is important to know the qualifying rules, which you can get from your local mortgage broker. At the time of writing this book, anyone looking to qualify for a mortgage must do so using the benchmark rate of 5.24% amortized over 25 years. So using our trusty Canadian Mortgage calculator we can determine that based on the yearly income of $60,000 the family could qualify for a mortgage of $252.000. So if your home were worth more than $252,000 then you would not want to put someone in the home that only makes $60,000 per year.

The second formula the banks use to qualify someone for a mortgage is the amount of their total monthly debt repayment. Here, the banks allow up to 40% of an individual's gross income to service the mortgage, taxes, and heat along with all other monthly payments like vehicles, lines of credit, and credit card or department store cards. Based on the $60,000 example used previously, the family would need to have their monthly payments being $2,000 or less per month to qualify.

Having a mortgage broker that understands rent to owns and is willing to help you with the qualification process is crucial. There are a lot of mortgage brokers out there who indicate they understand rent to owns and have processed them before, but in reality there aren't. Rent to owns account for less than 1% of the house sales in this country, so to find someone who truly understands what the lenders are looking for, which lenders will accept the contracts, what paperwork you are going to need to have documented and put together to process the sale at the end of the term isn't easy.

When I started doing RTOs back in 2009 I was introduced to a mortgage broker who was just in the process of setting up her own brokerage. As she was setting out starting her own business she took the time to find out what the "A" lenders, the big players like RBC, TD, BMO, CIBC, etc., required and how they required it in order to put the rent to own sale through. She also went to the "B" lenders, for people with lower credit score and higher risk individuals, to see which of them would process the rent to owns, which ones accepted the contracts as they were and which ones only accepted part of the contracts. She also went to the insurers of the mortgages, places like CMHC and Genworth to find out the same things. When it was all said and done she knew how to present the paperwork for her future clients to each lender in order to get the client qualified for the mortgage.

Since then she has gone on to teach her staff how to handle rent to owns and in my opinion is considered one of the best mortgage brokers in the country.

Not just because she deals with rent to owns but also handles the needs of our investors the same way. She looks at the big picture and the objectives of the investor; she knows and understands the lenders and what they will accept even before she starts finding lenders for the investors' purchases.

You are going to want to find a mortgage broker who understands rent to owns, like my mortgage broker does, and agrees to pre-qualify your tenant buyers in exchange for you bringing them potential future clients. You want to know from the mortgage broker if your tenant buyers could qualify to buy your home today if they had the full down payment and great credit. If the answer is yes, then you then move on to the second crucial piece of criteria, how long before they can qualify.

Credit Coaching

What most people don't know is that an individual can qualify for some of the best rates available within three years of being discharged from bankruptcy or consumer proposal. This is one of the biggest reasons you want to structure your rent to own for a time frame of three years. You want to make sure they are given enough time to get things straightened out.

It is important you connect with a certified credit coach and make it mandatory for the tenant buyers to meet with the coach initially during the application process so you can get the assessment of how long it will take to fix their credit. The role of the coach is to advise the tenant buyers what they need to do today as well as a strategy over the next three years to ensure they are on track to buy the home.

When I first started building this process back in 2009 I connected with a company that had representatives in their organization who were certified credit coaches. After several meetings we decided to work together. In reality they needed time to check me out to ensure they were partnering with someone that had a similar approach to helping people, the right morals and ethics. Once we agreed to work together we figured out a process when we would get applications from potential tenant buyers.

Up to this point in time I was getting a lot of people interested in rent to own and they would fill in the application if they were interested in getting into one of the properties. Now, we were starting to pre-qualify any and all individuals who wanted to get into a rent to own. So regardless of whether we had a home for them, if they wanted to get into a rent to own the first step was to get pre-qualified through our program. I noticed a substantial decrease in the number of people who followed through and filled in the application.

To be pre-qualified the tenant buyer must fill in the application, which then went to the mortgage broker and the credit coach. The mortgage broker was to review the information to determine what their maximum qualification amount was and the credit coach's role was to advise the client how long they need and what they needed to do to qualify. At the beginning the credit coaching company would call the tenant buyer's to set up meetings then report back to me after the meeting had taken place. What ended up happening was that people would not call the coach back for the meeting and they would miss meetings on a regular basis. There were also many times the coaches didn't know why the client was there in the first place.

When we first started sending people to the credit coach there was no fee, the company made money on other products and services they hoped to sell the clients during their time helping them, and the company called the tenant buyers to set up meetings. After some time the credit coaches realized they were putting in a lot of effort trying to contact and follow up with people who just weren't showing up.

At that point in time I instructed the credit coaching representatives that we will keep the process the same; however, they were to do nothing with the file at all if the tenant buyer didn't call to book an appointment. I shifted the responsibility to the tenant buyer to take control of their future and make them responsible for contacting the credit coach for a meeting. When this was done there was another drop in the number of people that actually filled in applications and sent them to us for processing.

Approximately nine months went by using this method of qualifying tenant buyers before the credit coaches decided to no longer offer the service as part of their core business. They were having tremendous success with some of their other products and services and decided to concentrate all their efforts on the ones that made them money immediately, which I don't blame them for doing. But before they announced they were no longer going to help me and the rest of the people conducting rent to owns, they did their own due diligence to find a replacement.

Their replacement is a credit coach who has written a book on credit and charges for his time, which I can respect. He makes his living doing nothing but consulting others on their credit and helping them get from where they are to where they need or want to be. He charges an hourly rate for his expertise, which rivals some lawyers. I have started collecting an upfront $500 application fee, which covers my time as well as the credit coach's time. If I can help the person get into a home I will credit the $500 towards their down payment, if I can't help them I will refund $250, which is my fee since I couldn't get them into a home.

Now, I've just gone and added another layer to the application process for my tenant buyers, which will decrease the numbers even further. But decreasing the numbers from 100 people per month showing interest to only five that complete the process to get things started immediately is ok. You see, every level of prequalification I've put in place eliminates more and more people who are not serious about fixing their situation and being able to buy a home at the end. The people who come through my process now are people who are committed to making it work, are going to care for the home and will pay their rent on time.

Having an abundance of homes makes it easier to help more people, which is one of the reasons I'm writing this book. I want to educate you, the home owner, on how to make more money on the sale of your home, while at the same time get more homes on the market for the people I put through my application process. Having a greater selection of properties available all the time will increase the number of people who will go through the application process.

You will want to connect with a credit coach and bring them onto your team to help you qualify the potential tenant buyers who want to rent to own your home. This is a very crucial step in the process and definitely one you do not want to skip.

You will want to advise any potential tenant buyers that it is mandatory for them to meet with the coaches before you consider them for the home. The bottom line here is that if they are not willing to pay the initial fee to work with an expert on their credit and meet with them at least once a year then I wouldn't even consider them. If they are not willing to invest a little time and money to fix their credit situation so they can buy the home at the end, why would you ever want to put them in your home?

I'm not going to get into too much detail about the credit situation other than this. If the tenant buyer was foreclosed on in the past, they will have to wait seven years after the foreclosure to get another mortgage. If the person is currently in consumer proposal or bankruptcy then they will have to finish out their term and get discharged, then they will need three years from that point to qualify for a mortgage. If the person is either already discharged or has never been through any of the above they can almost always qualify in three years or less. For me, it is important I know the basics like I just mentioned, but anything above that I leave to the experts. Just make sure you have a credit coach on your team and make it a mandatory part of your application process.

Of course you will also want to verify their employment and status at the company. Asking questions about them being late for work, what condition they keep their workspace and meeting deadlines can speak volumes about an individual. It is important to call their current landlord as well as the previous landlords. The current landlord may just want them out of the place and will say anything, but the previous landlord will typically tell you the truth. The most important thing to ask them is if they would ever rent to them again.

The screening process is one of the most crucial steps to ensuring you will have a successful rent to own. It is not a step you want to just brush over, it is one that you want to spend the majority of your time.

Step 5: Signing the Contracts:

Now that you have selected the person who is going to rent to own your home, it is time to get the contracts signed and collect some money. But first things first, you need contracts.

Getting access to tried, tested and proven rent to own contracts is not easy, and thinking you can just walk into your local real estate lawyer to have them whip you up a set probably isn't going to happen. That's because the majority of real estate lawyers are the straight transactional type, they deal with simple buy/sell deals.

When you are looking for a real estate lawyer to set up rent to own contracts, you are looking for a lawyer who is familiar with three specific things. The first is obvious; they need to know real estate law. The second is not so obvious, they need to know and understand the Property Act for their province while the third is even rarer, and they need to understand the provincial Residential Tenancy Act.

Good rent to own contracts have taken all three things into consideration and are vital should you ever end up in court. But the contracts themselves are not enough; you also need to prove that you did everything in your power to advise the tenant buyers of the risks, advised them to seek legal advice and prove that they fully understood what they were getting into and the ramifications if they defaulted on any aspect of the contracts. This in itself is a process and a very important one because everything you do here is like planning the divorce before you even get married.

The Contracts

It is important that your rent to own contracts include a variety of elements to protect yourself should anything happen and you end up in court. I am going to list a few of the things your lawyer needs to consider and why. Obviously I'm not a lawyer nor am I giving you any legal advice, I'm just passing on words of wisdom from my mentors and lawyers.

When it comes to rent to own or lease option contracts it is important to have two separate contracts, one for the lease and one for the option. It is also important that the individual giving the option is not the same person or entity that is leasing the home to the tenant buyer. I realize that seems strange but let me explain.

If you are the leasor, the person who is leasing the property to the tenant buyer, as well as the optionor, the person who has given the tenant buyer the option to purchase, and the person fails to pay the rent then going to the landlord and tenancy board is not going to enable you take action against the tenant to collect rent or evict them. All the tenant buyer has to say is they are in a rent to own with you and because the lease and the option are both in your name the person at the tenancy board will likely send you right to court, which can be a lengthy process.

If, however, you put your name as the optionor giving the tenant buyer the option to buy the home and opened up a company, such as a numbered company, and that was the company that was the leasor, the company that had the lease with the tenant buyer, then the transactions are seen completely separate. If you go to the Landlord and Tenant board for non-payment of rent and the tenant buyer says they have a RTO, your case should still be heard in the Tenancy Board because your company is just leasing the property to the tenant buyer and has nothing to do with giving them an option to purchase the home. You as the optionor and the company are seen as two separate entities.

With this type of arrangement it is much easier to get the people out of the home and get someone else in the property while you then go to court to take care of the option to purchase they have on the home.

When you set up your company to lease the property to the tenant buyer, you will need to have an agreement between yourself and your company. This agreement is a lease between you and your company, giving your company the ability to sub-lease the property. With this type of arrangement your company can lease the property for the actual costs, or whatever your accountant recommends. Typically, not always, you would want your corporation to incur the profits from the rental so any income is taxed at a much lower tax bracket. Not only that, you can claim all expenses regarding the home through the corporation, such as repairs, maintenance, advertising, your mileage and more. You really need to consult an accountant on the benefits of having a corporation.

Another reason for having your lease and your option coming from two separate entities has to do with the Property Act in some provinces. In Alberta, for example, there is a clause that will void an option contract and a lease contract if you have both contracts in your name. I recommend setting up two separate companies, one for the lease and one for the option, then give then lease the property to one company and option the property to the other company. You would then turn around and sublease the property to the tenant buyers from one company and option the company to the tenant buyers from the other company.

If you don't know what the act in your province says consult a lawyer who is familiar with the property act or just error on the side of caution and make sure the option and lease contracts come from different people or entities.

Here is the excerpt from the Property Act in Alberta.

Attornment clause

34(1) Every covenant, agreement, condition or stipulation that is contained in a mortgage or agreement for sale, or in any other instrument of any kind that is supplementary or collateral to a mortgage or agreement and whereby the mortgagor agrees or has agreed to become the tenant of the mortgagee or whereby the purchaser agrees or has agreed to become the tenant of the vendor, as the case may be, is void.

As the owner of the home, or as the investor who may be looking to sandwich lease the home, it is important to have different names as the leasor and the optionor or you could risk having the contracts voided and you may be forced to pay back the option money, should you ever end up in court.

When it comes to the lease the Landlord and Tenancy Act for your area will prevail. You want to have a lease that covers the basics of all leases such as the rent amount, security deposit, tenant's responsibility for utilities, inspections, care of premises, expectations for maintenance costs, tenant insurance, sub-letting, rules and regulations and right of entry to name a few. The important piece to remember is that this lease should never reference the option to purchase or rent to own in any way. Referencing the option to purchase agreement can cause you problems if you ever need to go to the tenancy board for eviction.

When it comes to the option contract you will want to make sure it abides by both the Property Act for your area as well as has things needed by the lenders. One of the biggest misconceptions is that your option contract must contain a clause where a portion of the money is refundable to the tenant buyer should they not buy the home in order to get CMHC insured. I can tell you straight out that this is not the case with an option contract, or the ones we use. Here is the clause from the CMHC website:

"Rent will only be accepted towards a down payment if it was acknowledged in a contractual agreement that includes the prepayment of equity on a monthly basis as part of an agreement to purchase. This option must involve only the monthly payment of an amount in excess of the market rent for that property. The original agreement should also contain some provision for a full (or partial) refund of that amount in the event that the prospective purchaser did not exercise this right to buy. The total amount of down payment to be credited to the borrower

may not be more than the sum of those monthly payments that exceeded the fair market rental for that property."

What does this mean?

1) It says "Rent will only be accepted towards a down payment..." We don't put any rent towards a down payment, we are charging as "Option Consideration" so this part doesn't apply

2) The tenant-buyer makes their payments to us in two separate checks. One check for "Rent" and another for "Monthly Option Consideration".

3) The rule says it "should" also contain some provision for a full (or partial) refund. This is not a "must", therefore we don't refund.

4) As the CMHC excerpt says the amount credited towards the down payment must be the portion above market rent. Looking back at section 2 of this chapter where we calculated the rent and the option payments you notice that we always took into consideration fair market rent and broke the total payment in two separate parts; rent and option consideration. So just check your numbers and ensure you're collecting the monthly money you want, and ensure it's in the fashion CMHC "wants".

The lenders and the insurers have approved the contracts we use every time the tenant buyer has fixed their credit where they are approved by "A" lenders. I give the credit to our lawyers for designing the contracts and my mortgage broker for understanding rent to own and what the lenders and insurers require.

Another important component of the option contract is that it must be fair and reasonable in the eyes of the judge. If, for example your contract indicated that the tenant buyer was going to lose their option the very first time they are one second late getting you their option payment is probably not going to go over well with the judge. You want to make sure that your option contract is there to protect you but does give a little leeway. Should you end up in court this will show the judge that you were more than fair. Obviously you don't want non-payment to drag on so set some limits.

Another strategy we employ is having the tenant buyers write in their own handwriting some of the key components of the contract on the back of the contract. Things such as what happens to their non-refundable option payment should they not pay as per the contract or exercise their option to buy the home and that they are responsible for repairs and maintenance below a certain dollar value.

You may also want to have agreements regarding pets, use of recreational items in the yard, smoke detectors, carbon monoxide detectors, illegal activity on the premises and agreeing to meet with the credit coach every 5-7 months just to name a few. Another thing I'm starting to implement is to video tape the tenant buyers doing a question and answer session where they say in their own words their understanding of the main pieces of the contract. These will go a long way if you should ever end up in court or they forget components of the agreements.

To go along with the rent to own contracts you will also require move in and move out inspection forms that you will want to walk through with the tenant buyer before they move into the property. It is advisable that you take as many photos of your house as possible while they are filling in the reports. While they are in the kitchen checking out the floors, walls, cupboards, ceilings, appliances, windows and doors you are taking pictures of everything so should the divorce happen, you have photographic proof of what the home looked like before they moved in. That way there is no dispute about damage.

Also, make sure you have a document signed by the tenant buyers indicating they have indeed sought out independent legal advice and under no circumstances did you or your representatives coerce them into the agreement.

A valuable piece of information to remember when you are signing contracts and doing the walk through has to do with the money. Upon signing all the documents it is expected you collect the initial option payment (down payment) as well as the rent, damage deposit and option for the first month. When doing so it is vital you request to have those in either bank draft or certified funds. Never accept a regular cheque and it is probably advisable not to accept cash because of the potential for money laundering.

Finally, the tenant is screened, contracts signed, walk through done and certified funds in hand. For most, they think everything is now done until the end when the tenant buyer buys or doesn't buy, but they are wrong.

Documentation During the Term:

Even though the majority of the work is done, there are still some administrative things that need to be done on a monthly and yearly basis. Having a system in place to handle things throughout the rent to own term can be the difference between a messy divorce and a dream anniversary.

You want to be documenting things for both the sale of the home at the end of the rent to own and the demise of the rent to own all together. You always hope for the best but plan for the worst.

Things you are going to want to track and have copies of when it comes time for the tenant buyer to purchase the home at the end of the rent to own. One of the most important things you want to track during the term of the rent to own is the tenant buyer's credit report. You will want them to provide you with a new copy, or you can have them give you authorization to pull a new copy, at least every six months. It would actually be best if you can have them see the credit coach every six months.

During this time you are going to want to see positive improvement and the score going up. A conversation with the mortgage broker or credit coach you are working with can help you determine if the tenant buyers are on track. A copy of their report as well as notes or comments from the mortgage broker and credit coach in the file is also advisable.

Another item you will need for the sale to go through is proof of payment. Every time you receive funds from the tenant buyer you want to document that by photocopying the front and back of every cheque or printing off the email transfer message, depending on how they send you the funds. You will also want to request a copy of the tenant buyer's bank statement the month prior to them giving you the down payment as well as the month they gave you the down payment. When it comes time to get a mortgage the lender is going to want verification of where the money came from for the down payment.

Documenting everything is crucial and doing things like photocopying cheques, both front and back before you deposit them, any and all communication between yourself and the tenant buyer, record any maintenance requests and when the work was done, documenting any late payments with the use of a 14 Day notice in Alberta or the equivalent in other provinces as well as charging and collecting late and NSF fees.

When it comes right down to it, if you ever end up in court the person with the best records, the person with the best paperwork trail, the person who can prove the other party knew the risks and consequences and can prove without a shadow of a doubt they have done everything in their power and to the letter of the law will usually end up being the one on the winning end of the judgment.

Closing on the Sale at the End

The wait is over, the tenant buyers have done everything they needed to do to repair their credit and you have helped them build up a minimum 5% documented down payment on the home. The next thing to do is sell them the home. This is where a mortgage broker experienced with rent to own is crucial. The manner in which the documentation is presented to the lenders will make all the difference in the world when it comes to closing on the sale.

Generally, it isn't a problem to have a lender agree to give the tenant buyer the mortgage; it is getting the mortgage insurer to insure the mortgage. If you aren't aware, any mortgage with less than a 20% down payment must be insured in Canada by one of the insurers such as CMHC or Genworth. Since the tenant buyer has had some issues with their credit the insurer wants to see everything cleared up on their bureau with about one year or clean credit since things have been cleared.

Having a mortgage broker and a real estate lawyer who is working with the tenant buyer and has knowledge of the rent to own industry is crucial at this point in time. I've met with my mortgage broker on many occasions over the last four years and there is a common conversation that keeps coming up. That is where she has been contacted by another mortgage broker somewhere in Canada that can't get the client approved through a rent to own so she has to come in and save the day by restructuring the information and presenting it in the appropriate manner in order to get the funding approved. Because of this she is starting to implement a fee to other mortgage brokers she has to help when saving a file.

Your real estate lawyer should have at least some knowledge of lease option contracts, or at least the premise of the contracts, so they are comfortable putting through the sale. For many it isn't so much the lawyer as their conveyancer who does the actual work. In reality, when the mortgage broker has financing approval the transaction for the lawyer is relatively simple and standard. The mortgage broker did all the heavy lifting, but you still need to have a lawyer who understands the premise of the lease option contracts.

Congratulations

Once you have completed the sale you can congratulate yourself on a job well done. You will have followed the steps to successfully turning your home into a rent to own, found qualified tenant buyers, took all the necessary precautions with the right documentation and put money in your pocket while helping a family become homeowners.

As I mentioned at the beginning of Chapter 9 I covered a lot of important information while reviewing the five steps you need to take. You will want to review the information in these chapters a few times, as well as the documentation included in the tools you received when you turned in your receipt at receipts@renttoownrevolution.com. You may want to watch the video before you re-read these two chapters to help you understand all of the information presented.

Turning your home into a rent to own is a complicated process. If after reviewing this information you feel like you would like some additional training or information in order to successfully take advantage to of the *Rent to Own Revolution*, then take a look at the next chapter. In Chapter 11 I outline some additional resources I created for those who may want to take full advantage of the rent to own system.

Chapter 11

ADDITIONAL RENT TO OWN SERVICES

"The true sign of intelligence is not knowledge but imagination."--Albert Einstein

Up to this point I have shared with you my experiences and stories over the past four years of building a successful rent to own business. I have walked you through the five reasons to turn your home into a rent to own and showed you how the money is made in this business, money you can tap into yourself. I have even walked you through the steps you need to structure your very own rent to own and by sending in the receipt of your book purchase to receipts@renttoownrevolution.com you receive the rent to own workbook and some training videos that walk you through the 5 reasons to turn your home into a Rent To Own and how to calculate how much money you can make on your home, a $497 Value, absolutely free just by emailing your receipt to me.

As you are well aware, just knowing how to rent to own your home is only part of the equation, finding lawyers to draw up contracts, mortgage brokers and credit coaches who know what they are doing, marketing and promoting your home, managing the documentation throughout the term of the rent to own, heck even managing the entire process can make some of you decide not to bother turning your home into a rent to own. That is why, when I decided to write and launch this book I wanted to make sure I didn't leave you just hanging. I wanted to make sure you had at least one place you know you could turn for help.

My role in this chapter is not to pressure you into using any of my services, my role is to educate you of the services I have worked over four years to perfect as I worked my way to becoming a trusted authority in the real estate investing strategy of RTO. I am very confident I gave you enough information throughout the book that you can go out on your own and find the things you need or do it yourself. I just wanted to give you some options should you want to save time and energy.

Do It Yourself Rent To Own Program

The workbook and the training series will walk you through establishing the numbers you are going to be asking for when turning your home into a rent to own. What your end maximum and minimum prices are going to be, how much your basic rent is, what is the least you will accept for an initial option payment and how much the tenant buyers will need to pay extra per month to ensure they have the minimum 5% down payment when it comes time to purchase the home. The program will also walk you through, in detail, all 5 steps in the Step by Step process from chapters 9 and 10.

For more information on the Do It Yourself Rent To Own Program visit

http://0s4.com/r/RTODYS

or Scan

Marketing System for Your Home

I know what it takes to attract tenant buyers; I've been doing it very successfully for the past four years. I also know marketing; specifically Internet based marketing and getting people to take action. With my program we create a complete marketing system for your home, which will include its own dedicated webpage, QR code, Opt Ins, voice message for interested callers, a pdf brochure you can print off, possibly a local number they can call or text to get information, a sign and your home will be featured on the ioffersolutions.com and ioffersolutions.ca websites for maximum exposure.

We will also create a Search Engine Optimized video from the pictures of your home and distribute it across the Internet to get maximum exposure. The signs, videos, website, brochures will all focus on collecting the person's name, email and mobile number so we can have a series of automated responses set to be delivered to them and we can use the system to co-ordinate an open house for maximum exposure.

You will also receive the copy you can cut and paste into craigslist or kijiji to help promote your rent to own home. It will also encourage people to get into your lead funnel so we can follow-up automatically. For more information on the Marketing System or pricing information please visit

http://0s4.com/r/RTOMS

or Scan

Application Service

Do you want to make sure you are doing everything possible to set your tenant buyers up for success? Would you like the opportunity to work with my personal mortgage broker and credit coach to assess the people looking to rent to own your home? As I have discussed throughout this book it is vital to have a mortgage broker and a credit coach involved with the tenant buyers right from the start all the way through to the very end. Having access to individuals who have established themselves as trusted authorities in their fields, as well as experts when it comes to RTOs will save you a tremendous amount of time searching out your own qualified individuals.

My credit coach and mortgage broker work with individuals across the country via phone, fax, Skype and email. You don't have to be in the same city to have your rent to own credit assessment; you just need to send in the application to get it processed. The cost of the service is one cost you want to pass on to your tenant buyers as they are getting their information assessed and having consultations. Remember, the mortgage broker and credit coach earn their living working with individuals just like your future tenant buyers, so just like any business, their time is valuable. To find out more about getting access to my personal credit coach and mortgage broker then visit

http://0s4.com/r/APPLIC

or Scan

Contract Service

In the last chapter I gave you a lot of great information with respect to things your contracts should contain as well as why. But still, there is so much more that goes into rent to own contracts than just the items I listed in the chapter. This is why I've decided to make the exact same contracts I use available to you.

I work with a lawyer in Alberta who is considered to be an expert in rent to owns, so much so that one of the largest real estate investing training organizations in North America sought him out to consult on the sample lease option contracts used in teaching the lease option course, as well as having him teach a course on asset protection. I consult with him regularly to ensure there are no changes in either the Property Act or Landlord and Tenancy Acts that I need to be aware of. If so we make changes to the contracts to reflect the new changes.

Let me be clear, I am not selling contract templates; I am offering a contract service where you will get contracts created specifically for your home, your tenant buyer and the term required. Even though the contract templates themself have been created by a lawyer and have been prepared for your situation by a legal assistant, it is still your responsibility to take the contracts to your local lawyer to review and to help you understand all aspects associated with the contracts. The cost of using our service is much less then the cost for me to have the contracts created initially.

When you use our contract service we are also going to create a customized 50+ page homeowners manual, which contains the following;

1. Automatic Payment Plan Authorization
2. Cold Weather Checklist
3. Credit and Payment History Letter
4. Fire Extinguisher Agreement
5. Important Telephone Numbers
6. Lead-Based Paint Hazards Disclosure
7. Move-in Inspection
8. Moving Checklist
9. Moving Expense Checklist
10. New Resident Information Sheet
11. New Resident Neighborhood Information
12. No Criminal Activity Agreement
13. Apparent Conditions Disclosure
14. Occurrence Receipt
15. Pet Agreement
16. Preventing Mold Growth
17. Recreational Items Release Agreement
18. Tenant Lease Agreement
19. Tenant Option Contract
20. Notes on Credit
21. Renter's Insurance Reminder Letter
22. Hand Written Script

23. Request for Maintenance Form
24. Resident Locked Out Form
25. Rules and Regulations
26. Smoke Detector Agreement
27. Suspicious Behavior/Activity Report (For your safety)
28. Utility Transfer Sheet
29. Warm Weather Checklist
30. Certificate of Independent Legal Advice and Acknowledgement
31. Affidavit and Caveat Forbidding Registration
32. Welcome Letter
33. New Home Manual Receipt and Checklist

For more information about our contract service visit

http://0s4.com/r/RTOCS

or Scan

Monthly Online Property Management and Document Tracking System

Whether you are just renting your home or turning your home into a rent to own, documentation during the term is crucial. This is where so many homeowners will drop the ball and could end up with someone in their home for a lengthy period of time without collecting any income. For most homeowners, they just don't know the rules of the lenders when it comes to the option and purchase and the rules of the Landlord and Tenancy board when it comes to the lease.

Our online system contains a portal where you and your tenant buyer can go into and leave messages. For example, the tenant needs to get come repairs done to the home that are over the allotted value in their contract they would go into the portal and leave a message for the owner. An email is generated and sent to the owner advising them there is some work that needs to be done. Obviously if it is urgent, a phone call would be advisable, however it is very difficult to track phone calls and conversations, but with our system we can have all communication in one place.

Another benefit of the service is the documents and reports. Should, for example, your tenant not pay rent on the first, then on the second you need to be posting a notice on the door. We can automatically generate the reports you need; along with the steps you need to take in order to ensure you are following the letter of the Landlord and Tenant Act. For most homeowners they are not aware of the steps, but we are. You can benefit from our knowledge and expertise when it comes to managing properties.

I am currently in negotiations with a broker to come on board with the company so we can give you the ability to collect money from your tenant using pre authorized debit and we can have the money sent directly to your account. Combining the collection of the rent and the option will automatically give us the ability to generate the reports on the 2nd of the month automatically without you having to contact us and let us know the funds weren't there. You will still be responsible for contacting the tenant buyer, posting notices, etc. but we will aid you in preparing all the documentation.

At least four times a year you are going to want to inspect the property. With our system we can send you a reminder when you should do your inspection and prepare the paperwork you need to post on the door advising the tenant buyer you are coming in the property as well as the inspection report. Once the inspection report has been completed you can upload it into the system to keep on file with the rest of your information.

For more information about our Monthly Online Property Management and Document Tracking System visit

http://0s4.com/r/RTOPMS

or Scan

Rent To Own Service - By Rent to Own Revolution

For many of you reading this book you may like the idea of turning your home into a rent to own and definitely see the advantages and benefits of doing so. Even with the free training program, step by step system and tools, along with the paid services to ensure you are doing everything the way it should be done, many of you just don't want to, or don't have the time to do the work. Many of you would just like someone else to come in and put it all together for you.

Our rent to own service is available in areas where we have a licensed representative. Right from the beginning our representatives will come in and assess the home, calculate the rent to own options for the tenant buyer, organize all the marketing of the home, screen prospective tenant buyers, put them through the application process, show the home, conduct the walk through inspection, sign the contracts with the tenant buyers and manage the project right to the very end up to and including the sale of the home.

For more information about our rent to own service and our fees visit

http://0s4.com/r/SERVIC

or Scan

Guaranteed Rent to Own Program

The majority of the homeowners absolutely love this service because they rent to own the home to my company or one of our associates, so they know they have someone to manage the property, they never have to worry about vacancy or even repairs. They know that if the home isn't purchased at the end of the rent to own term I will hand it back in the same condition less normal wear and tear.

Another reason homeowner's love this option is because they have zero upfront costs. They don't have to pay for marketing, contracts, tenant buyer assessments or monthly tracking. Typically within 60 days from when we sign contracts they are starting to get their rent cheques, regardless of whether we have found a tenant buyer in the home or not.

However, in using this service you don't get to capitalize on all the benefits of the rent to own. Since my company is taking a risk in renting your place and having the option to buy with the hopes of putting in a good family, there are things that can happen during the term, which I have pointed out throughout this book.

We pay the homeowner slightly below fair market rent, guaranteed, filled or vacant and have a set purchase price at the end of the term based on today's fair market value of the home. We collect and keep all the option money, the difference between what we charge for rent and what we pay you for rent, and we benefit if the home sells for more than our guaranteed purchase price with you.

You get zero vacancy for 36 months guaranteed. We cover all repairs and maintenance under $1000 per instance, keeping your expenses to a minimum, you benefit from the mortgage pay down during the term of the rent to own and you can still refinance and use RRSP's to gain access to some of your equity if needed.

This program is the preferred program for our investors. Instead of creating companies, setting up unanimous shareholder agreements or joint venture agreements our investors like the ability to just buy homes for us to put into our guaranteed program. We limit the risk to them substantially. As mentioned, this is a great method to generate additional money so you can go out and buy the long term buy rent and hold properties that will generate long term wealth for you.

For more information about our guaranteed rent to own program and our fees visit

http://0s4.com/r/GRNTEE

or Scan

Rent To Own Revolution Licensed Agent - Biz Opp

Are you a real estate investor, Realtor or just someone interested in becoming a licensed agent for Rent to Own Revolution in your area? Would you like to capitalize on the revolution and help both homeowners and tenant buyers alike? The system comes with your own marketing system for generating new clients as well as looking after all the company leads generated for your area. Along with the system you get in depth training and coaching support.

For more information about our Rent To Own Revolution Licensed Agent, the opportunity and the fees visit

http://0s4.com/r/BIZOPP

or Scan

While we may have come to the end of our story, the *Rent to Own Revolution* is far from over. I offered you a lot of information in this book and you may want to read it again to make sure you understand everything I have explained to you. You may also want to have access to the free tools while you read the different chapters to help you gain better insight into some of the material I offer about converting your home to a rent to own.

In the first chapter I asked you to keep one question in mind while you were reading this book: When am I going to join the Revolution?

This is the right question to ask. Not *if* you are going to join but *when*. The traditional method of selling your home isn't working and the alternatives of renting your home or selling it on your own can lead to some expensive problems. In this book I outlined the benefits of the Rent to Own Revolution method for homeowners, tenant buyers, and real estate investors.

Homeowners benefit from using this solution because:

- It eliminates Realtor fees and tenant expenses
- You get zero vacancy for the length of the term
- You eliminate paying the prepayment fees to get out of your mortgage early
- You have someone else pay for repairs and maintenance of up to $1,000 per instance
- You get to let someone else pay down your mortgage, which gives you more money at the end.

- You make money each month from cash flow
- You sell your home at appreciated value

Tenant Buyers benefit from this solution because:

- It gives you the opportunity to qualify as a homeowner, which may not occur using the traditional method of buying a home
- It provides you the ability to take the time you need to repair your credit while you make payments toward owning a home
- You can avoid the less than ethical companies who are only looking out for their profit and don't care about helping you
- By completing the process and obtaining a mortgage for your new home you are making an important step for your future

Real estate investors benefit from this solution because:

- Investing in real estate is more secure than other forms of investment
- You can use this method without using your own money
- It eliminates many of the headaches of traditional rentals or sales
- You can duplicate the process and achieve the same results
- You can use the cash flow you earn for investing in other rent to own homes

I also showed you the steps you would need to take in order to be successful in the rent to own process. I outlined a method you can use if you need the equity from your home, how to determine the selling price of your home, and how to market your home as a rent to own. I also explained the best method for screening tenant buyers and the documents you will need from before the tenant buyers move in to the day of the closing.

I pulled back the curtain and allowed you to see the entire rent to own process in a way that few rent to own companies are willing to show you. I cast a light in the dark corners of the business to reveal how the less than ethical organizations attempt to take money from investors, home owners and tenant buyers. I also supplied you with all of the tools you need to help make rent to own a success.

But I can only show you the way; the next step is up to you. So, once again I ask you:

Where do you want to be when the storm hits and the revolution starts? Do you want to be poised to take advantage of the situation and benefit or do you want to continue doing what you have always done because it is comfortable and what you know?

Now that you understand the process and have the tools you need to succeed are you ready to join the revolutionaries?

I hope that you are, and I stand ready to assist you in any way I can to help you earn a profit by turning your home into a rent to own.

I wish you success in this and all of your ventures. And I hope to see you taking part in the *Rent to Own Revolution*.

Remember....

To Join the Rent To Own Revolution Member's Area FREE and get accesses to all the latest updates and resources.

Text your name and email to 780-800-7464

OR Visit http://0s4.com/r/RTOMA

OR Scan the QR code

Appendix

i

Frequently Asked Questions

I have included a list of questions that tenant buyers often ask when they are considering the rent to own path to homeownership. These questions are ones you may need to answer if you are looking to turn your home into a rent to own. I hope the answers I provide will help you.

Lease Options FAQ #1

Question:
What Exactly is Rent to Own?

Answer:
It is a solution that bridges the gap between renting and buying. Rent to own provides people with the opportunity to enjoy their homes as a homeowner would, even though they may not currently qualify for conventional financing or have a large down payment to put towards a home purchase. When you rent to own a home, you do not have to qualify for a mortgage, but you are able to enjoy many of the benefits of home ownership.

Rent to own combines some aspects of renting a home and some of purchasing one. For example, it is similar to purchasing a home because a down payment is required, and it is similar to renting a home because there is a rent schedule.

One important thing to keep in mind is that – unlike a typical rental situation – a portion of your monthly payment goes towards the down payment that will be required when you obtain a mortgage to complete the future purchase of your home.

Don't have 5% down payment? You can still benefit with a rent to own. One important thing to keep in mind is that – unlike a typical rental situation – a portion of your monthly payment goes towards the down payment that will be required when you obtain a mortgage to complete the future purchase of your home.

Even if your credit is bruised you can benefit from a rent to own. We will help you restore your credit during the term of the rent to own, as well as help you build your down payment over the term of the rent to own.

Lease Options FAQ #2

Question:
Will I Have to Qualify for a Loan?

Answer:
We will work with you throughout the process to help you rebuild your credit. We also help you amass your minimum 5% down payment over the term of the rent to own. You will still need to qualify for our Rent to Own Home program, but we create a win-win situation and set you up for success right from the very beginning.

We also bring in two other vital team members. A mortgage broker to tell us how much you qualify for and a certified credit coach to tell us how long the term needs to be.

As an added service, we will set up quarterly meetings between ioffersolutions, your mortgage broker and credit coach to discuss your progress. By doing so, you will receive the joys of home ownership without qualifying for a mortgage today; even if your credit is bruised you can still get into a rent to own.

Lease Options FAQ #3

Question:
Can I Rent to Own if I Have Bad Credit?

Answer:
Part of the purpose of our rent to own program is to allow people the time they need to improve their credit ratings and prepare to qualify for a mortgage. We understand that things happen and believe that something like a bankruptcy, foreclosure, divorce or other event that could negatively affect credit ratings should not automatically bar people from the chance to experience home ownership.

It is for this exact reason we have you work with an independent certified credit coach who truly wants to help you succeed in home ownership. The credit coach will review your credit report and determine the length of time required to raise your credit score to a point where the banks will qualify you for a mortgage.

They will then work with you to fix any credit issues you may have and give you very specific step by step instructions to move closer to home ownership

Lease Options FAQ #4

Question:
How Much is the Down Payment?

Answer:
That really depends on the home you choose and your ability to pay. The bank usually requires a minimum of 5% down. For a Rent to Own, it will typically be three months' rent or 2% - 3% of purchase price.

An example is for a $300,000 home, the bank will require you to put 5% down, which comes out to $15,000. With a rent to own, you would be looking at 2-3%, which is $6,000-9,000.

Another advantage of a rent to own is that rent to own companies typically allow you other methods of paying for the down payment. Some things that rent to own companies can accept include assets such as land, RV's, ATV's, jewelry, vehicles and even labor if you are a handy person! This will have to be documented just like the banks, but it will provide you with extra flexibility as to where you can get the money from.

Lease Options FAQ #5

Question:
What if I Don't Have the Full Down Payment Upfront?

Answer:
This is actually often the case, so rest assured that we are here to help and have many suggestions to help you obtain the initial down payment needed, as well as the rest of the down payment you will need when you purchase your home later on.

That really depends on the home you choose and your ability to pay. The bank usually requires a minimum of 5% down. For a Rent to Own, it will typically be three months' rent or 2% - 3% of purchase price.

An example is for a $300,000 home, the bank will require you to put 5% down, which comes out to $15,000. With a Rent to Own, you would be looking at 2-3%, which is $6,000-9,000. If you have $9,000 available today for your rent to own, the remaining left to meet the bank's minimum of 5% would be $6,000. This will accumulate during the number of years in your rent to own term.

Another advantage of a rent to own is that rent to own companies typically allow you other methods of paying for the down payment. Some things that rent to own companies can accept include assets such as land, RV's, ATV's, jewelry, vehicles and even labor if you are a handy person! This will have to be documented just like the banks, but it will provide you with extra flexibility as to where you can get the money from.

Lease Options FAQ #6

Question:
How Much of My Monthly Rent Goes Towards My Down Payment?

Answer:
The amount of your monthly rent that goes towards your down payment depends on two things: The price of the home and your initial down payment.

When paying a mortgage, the majority of the payment goes towards interest. Principle paid down is very little in the first 10 years of a mortgage.

An example is for a $300,000 home, the bank will require you to put 5% down, which comes out to $15,000. With a rent to own, you would be looking at 2-3%, which is $6,000-9,000. If you have $9,000 available today for your rent to own, the remaining left to meet the bank's minimum of 5% would be $6,000. This will accumulate during the number of years in your rent to own term.

With a mortgage of $300,000 at an interest rate of 6% to be amortization over 30 years, your payment would come out to $1,750 per month. In this case, you are really only paying down $150 per month on the principal. In a rent to own case, you would need to make up the $6,000 during the rent to own term. If we assume that the length of the rent to own is 36 months, we can start to calculate how much of the monthly rent goes towards your down payment.

We take the remaining down payment required and divide by the number of months to give us the rent credit required per month. In this case, it would be $6,000 divided by 36 months, which comes out to $166.67.

Lease Options FAQ #7

Question:
What are Some Reasons My Application Would not be Approved?

Answer:
There are six reasons why your application would not be approved. The first reason is a lack of down payment. The second reason is that the house is located in a very rural area or is very specialized such as a farm. The third reason is that you chose a house that needs a lot of work. The fourth reason is if your current length of employment is shy of the minimum requirement. The fifth reason is if your current level of income cannot support the monthly payments required. And the final reason is if you are not meeting the deadlines with documentation or funds and or missing meetings with your credit coach.

Lease Options FAQ #8

Question:
What is the Price of a Home on a Rent to Own?

Answer:
The answer would depend on two things: The price of the home today and the area the home is located in. Over time, all homes appreciate, and that is a good thing for everyone. However, the rate of appreciation differs in different areas of the country. The CMHC average in Canada has been 4.5% per year, and this is what we use to establish the price at the beginning and guaranteed as part of the rent to own contract. Even if the home is worth more, take the current fair market value of the home and factor in the estimated appreciation for each year of the rent to own contract.

Lease Options FAQ #9

Question:
What if I Change My Mind and Decide Not to Buy the Home?

Answer:
When you are renting to own, choose a home that suits your needs for the long term. Now, we realize things can happen such as marital status or family status change, job relocation, and other things. If you had gone with a bank, and you decide that you don't want the home anymore, they would issue a foreclosure on your record that would last seven years. The banks can also sue you for any losses they incur.

With a rent to own, you get to walk away with no blemish to your credit. That is because with a rent to own you have the option to buy or not buy. You would only lose your option consideration as it is non-refundable. Another advantage is that you get to move on without additional consequences, even if that means we may be stuck with a property we never wanted.

Lease Options FAQ #10

Question:
Are There any Other Fees or Costs?

Answer:
On a rent to own, you make monthly rent and option payments. You will also be responsible for paying your own utilities, such as heat, water, electricity and other bills such as phone and cable. As with any rental, you will need to have and maintain your tenant insurance for the term of the rent to own. This is to protect yourself from any damages that may incur on your belongings. You will not need to make separate payments for things like property taxes or condo fees (if applicable). This will be taken care of by the owner, until you choose to exercise your option to buy.

If you wish to paint, decorate or remodel, you will be responsible for those costs. Note that all improvements require approval from the landlord or owner and must be accompanied by appropriate permits. Typically, you will also be responsible for all repairs and maintenance of the property under $500 or $1000, while the owner will be responsible for anything above that.

Just remember, rent to owns contains both aspects of renting, as well as aspects of home ownership.

ii

Should Ask Questions

Here is a list of questions that I recommend tenant buyers should ask when they are considering entering into a rent to own agreement with an individual homeowner or rent to own company. These are questions you should be prepared to answer when you rent your home for three years and then sell it to tenant buyers.

Lease Options SAQ #1

Question:
How do You Determine if I can Qualify within the Rent to Own term?

Answer:
Most rent to own companies work on behalf of the home owner and may only have a set period of time to rent to own the home. If this is the case, it is vital you know exactly how long you need to qualify. Never get into a rent to own without knowing how much time you need to qualify for the mortgage.

A good and reputable rent to own company should have a strategy or process to determine how long it is going to take to repair your credit. They should be working with both mortgage brokers and credit coaches, otherwise, you should research this yourself prior to seeking a rent to own home.

Know how much you qualify for, as well as how long it will take for you to qualify. You should also have a specific game plan laid out for fixing your credit. The minimum amount of time will depend on the answers you get from the credit coaches and the mortgage brokers. It is possible to find rent to own properties with options of up to five years.

If the rent to own company is not having you qualified with a mortgage broker for your limit, nor a credit coach to determine how long it will take to qualify for a mortgage then you are putting yourself at risk. If the company truly cared about you qualifying at the end of the term they would put you through this process at the beginning.

To sum it up, it truly does depend. It depends on your current situation and what the credit coach and mortgage broker say you need. You then take that information and find a rent to own home that meets your budget and time frame.

Lease Options SAQ #2

Question:
Can the Option be Extended if I Can't Obtain Financing?

Answer:
If you have been working with a certified credit coach and a mortgage broker, you will know how long it will take for you to qualify for your rent to own. Based on that information, you are going to only get into a rent

to own situation you know you can qualify for and not get into a term shorter than you need.

If something happens to your situation during your time in the rent to own, such as losing your job unexpectedly, and it now prevents you from qualifying, it is up to the rent to own company and or the home owner if they extend the option period.

The homeowner the rent to own company is working for may not want to extend the term, so they may have to find an investor to purchase the property in order to extend the contract.

They are under no obligation to extend the term, nor would they ever start writing all the "What if" scenarios into the contract that could come up in your life. Always keep in mind you should be working with a credit coach and mortgage broker to obtain financing from the very beginning.

If you were not following through with your commitment to work with the mortgage broker or the credit coach then the home owner and the rent to own company should not be penalized for lack of follow through on your part should you not continue working with the credit coach and mortgage broker.

If you can't qualify because you didn't follow through with your commitment to work with the credit coach and mortgage broker, then you can be assured there is a good chance the option will not get extended.

Lease Options SAQ #3

Question:
If the Home Declines in Value, do I Have any Protection?

Answer:
Yes, you have the ability to walk away from the home. You would lose your option, but walking away will not affect your credit. Remember, the home owner or rent to own company are still stuck with the home!

However, most homeowners choose to either extend the option in hopes that home prices will rise or lower the price of the home. Remember, the home owners or rent to own companies can't sell the home to anyone else for what they want or need to sell the home for, so it is in their best interest to extend the term with you or lower the price.

It is up to the home owner or rent to own company which option they choose to go with. Lowering the price may mean selling at a loss, which most are not willing to do.

If you choose to renegotiate, you should be armed with information about the cost of home values and the prospectus for the future of your type of home and your neighbourhood. Keep in mind the home owner or rent to own company are still in control and have no obligations, however most would continue working with you provided there were no issues in the past.

Lease Options SAQ #4

Question:
What Happens if the Home Owner Experiences a Foreclosure?

Answer:
If the home owner has financial issues, this is a serious and real possibility.
You would either need to be in a position to purchase the home at that point in time, negotiate with the home owner to take over payments to pay them directly, plus you would need to pay off the outstanding arrears, or you could see if you could get another party to purchase the home and continue on with the rent to own.

If you are unable to make any of that happen, then there is a good chance you will lose the option consideration you have into the property, as well you will need to find a new place to live.

As for rent to own companies, who work on behalf of home owners, their interests remain protected. Many times the rent to own companies will step in and make the payments on behalf of home owners to ensure the rent to own goes through. This would mostly depend upon your payment history with that property.

Typically, the rent to own company has a caveat on the property, so they are made aware of the owner's financial trouble before the home goes into foreclosure. Most times they will fix the issue and you never knew there was a problem.

As long as you keep your payments current and up to date, a reputable rent to own company will ensure the owner's payments are up to date. Rent to own companies typically get paid when the house sells so they want to protect their interest.

Lease Options SAQ #5

Question:
How Can I Make Sure the Home Owner is Paying the Mortgage?

Answer:
If you are dealing directly with a home owner and not a rent to own company you will want to ensure you register your option to purchase on title. You will be notified by the bank if the owner has not been paying the mortgage and
the bank is threatening to take over the property.

This allows you to learn about the property owner's payment status and will protect your interest in case the home owner goes into default. If you are dealing with a rent to own company, they will not allow you to register your interest as they have already registered theirs on the home owner's title.

Most rent to own companies have a clause in their contracts indicating the
option to purchase you have with them will be null and void should you register a caveat.

Your recourse with a rent to own company would be to pursue legal action against them should the house go into foreclosure.

Lease Options SAQ #6

Question:
Who is Responsible for Home Repairs?

Answer:
This is an answer you must find out before entering the rent to own agreement.
Usually the tenant is responsible for smaller repairs, while the property owner is responsible for any repair over $500 or $1000 per instance.

It is in your best interest to pay for a home inspection prior to entering into a rent to own contract. This would be the time to discover if the home has any major issues.

As with any home, you should make certain that there are no immediate concerns that may require a significant financial investment.
If you do find problems with the home, check and double check the agreement so that you can learn which party is responsible.

Lease Options SAQ #7

Question:
What is the Difference Between Dealing with an Owner or a Rent to Own Company?

Answer:
There is a very big difference between dealing with a homeowner just trying to sell their home and a company that specializes in rent to owns. Generally a homeowner does not know what it takes to get

someone qualified to purchase a home through a rent to own.

They think that selling their home through a rent to own will stop the bleeding with respect to their mortgage payment or they feel they will get substantially more for their home selling it using this method. Since the home owner can get above market rents, sell it for an appreciated value and get a down payment from the tenants, it can be an attractive option for them to try and structure the rent to own on their own.

These are the same reasons shady investors get into rent to own business. They take money with no desire or knowledge on how to get you qualified for a mortgage. In the end they have your money and you do not have a home.

Dealing with a rent to own company that specializes in structuring rent to owns, day in and day out is a completely different experience. A good rent to own company builds its business on referrals, has a process for ensuring you get qualified, partners with certified credit coaches and mortgage brokers, is up to date on all the CMHC regulations and makes sure all the appropriate paperwork and contracts are in place.

If you are thinking about getting into a rent to own and the person or company does not offer all the above mentioned then I would question if they truly want to see you succeed.

Lease Options SAQ #8

Question:
What are some of the risks or disadvantages to doing a lease option?

Answer:
There are a few disadvantages to getting into a rent to own, and anyone telling you otherwise is not being forth coming. The first would be that you are responsible for repairs and maintenance of the home. The best way to protect yourself and know exactly what you are getting into is to spend the $400-500 and have a home inspection completed prior to signing the contracts. This could save you thousands down the road.

A second risk, which we discussed in some of the other videos, is that the home may not have appreciated as much as predicted and be worth less than the contract price. You need to know what is going to happen if this is the case. There are many investors who will ask you to pay the difference, and why would you pay more for a house then it is worth. It is important you know today's FMV of the home and the average appreciation for the area based on CMHC stats to determine if the end price is in line. If it is, ask about the strategy should something happen to the economy and the house prices stay stagnant or not rise as high as predicted.

A third disadvantage is that you will require all renovations, painting or upgrades to the property be approved by the rent to own company or the owner.

This can sometimes feel like a hassle and if your tastes differ from the rent to own company or owner then you may not get approved on some of the things you want to do.

And lastly, you are typically paying a higher monthly payment then if you were just renting or you actually owned the house. This is because there is an additional amount required to be paid each month to build up your down payment. If you had the full 5% needed then the monthly payment would not be as high, however most don't have the full 5% required and need the forced savings the rent to own provides.

I can't just leave it with disadvantages; there are many advantages as well so I'm just going to run through a few of them. Get into the house you want right now – you don't have to wait the 2-3 years and you are putting a portion of your payment towards the future purchase of the home.

There is a set purchase price, so should there be a large jump in the house prices your end purchase price is locked in and you get to take advantage of the extra equity.
And lastly the additional payment each month forces you to get into the habit of saving, so when you purchase the home we hope you will continue with the habit to better your financial position.

Lease Options SAQ #9

Question:
Can I Have a Copy of the Contracts so I Can Review them?

Answer:

The answer should be yes. If you are considering getting into a rent to own and have gone through all the steps required, such as meeting with the mortgage broker and credit coach and you are set to go, you should always ask for a set of all the paperwork to review a few days prior to signing.

A good reputable rent to own company would not just encourage this but require you to seek legal advice. They should be advising you of all the risks you would encounter should you fail to pay the rent on time, not pay the rent, not maintain the home or not be able to purchase the home at the end of the term.

You should be hearing the exact same thing from your rent to own company as you hear from the lawyer. Remember, there are risks to everything you do and we can't account for every what if scenario that could happen. And, it is important to know what you are getting into, as well as, the advantages and disadvantages.

One thing you should know, which you will never be told by the bank. The risks of a rent to own are far less than the risks you take when you sign a mortgage with the bank. If you default with the bank you lose the house, typically all your equity, even if you have 20-30% once the banks and lawyers take all their fees if they foreclose on you and ruin your credit for seven years. You default on a rent to own and you have generally lost less than 5% of the down payment and your credit is still intact! So make sure you get a copy of the contracts, get them reviewed, and know the risks as well as the comparable risks to a traditional mortgage.

References

Martin Luther King Quote - http://ourrevolution.co/2012/08/21-inspirational-quotes-about-changing-the-world/

Graph p21 - www.theEconomicAnalyst.com

Quote from Freaconomics p28
http://www.cbc.ca/news/canada/story/2010/02/11/f-vp-keller.html

Revolution Quote p30 http://www.thefreedictionary.com/revolution

Shirley Chisholm quote p38
http://www.goodreads.com/author/show/142616.Shirley_Chisholm

Marcus Cicero, William J. Bennett, Ellie Rodriguez quote p64
http://www.truesarasota.com/true-sarasota-blog/sarasota-real-estate-facts-and-tips/quotes/home-and-homeownership

Jarod Kintz quote p91
http://www.goodreads.com/author/show/4157885.Jarod_Kintz

graph on p103 MSN Money.com

CRA Definition p106 IT-419R2 at http://www.cra-arc.gc.ca/E/pub/tp/it419r2/

Mark Twain quote p120
http://www.brainyquote.com/quotes/quotes/m/marktwain164246.html#yQ2mymJTHlqtlBsC.99

Ralph Waldo Emerson pg137 - http://www.movemequotes.com/top-10-giving-back-quotes/

Anne Isabella Ritchie pg139 http://www.phrases.org.uk/meanings/give-a-man-a-fish.html

Casey Stengel quote Engel pg 144
http://quotationsbook.com/quote/3760/#sthash.zepwR7BO.MvvzPPud.dpbs

Dido Armstrong quote pg 160
http://www.brainyquote.com/quotes/keywords/rent_4.html#8j3eOKUr5zYkgQoc.99

Danny Boyle quote pg 177
http://www.brainyquote.com/quotes/keywords/cash_2.html#GVlpi0l8YpgO6uGm.99

John C Maxwell quote pg 193
http://epicinspirationalquotes.com/#ixzz2eVMTqpIu

CMHC Research pg 198
https://www03.cmhc-schl.gc.ca/catalog/productList.cfm?cat=63&lang=en&fr=1372960372250

B. R. Ambedkar quote pg 213
http://www.brainyquote.com/quotes/keywords/thorough.html#w8WhIRBVSBxjImAV.99

Property Act Alberta Attornment clause pg 229
http://www.qp.alberta.ca/1266.cfm?page=L07.cfm&leg_type=Acts&isbncln=0779749758&display=html

Albert Einstein quote pg 239
http://www.brainyquote.com/quotes/authors/a/albert_einstein.html

Made in the USA
Charleston, SC
23 October 2014